THE LIFE AND DEATH

OF

Mary Magdalene.

Early English Text Society.

Extra Series, No. LXXVIII.

1899.

THE LIFE AND DEATH

OF

Mary Magdalene,

A LEGENDARY POEM IN TWO PARTS,
ABOUT A.D. 1620,

BY

THOMAS ROBINSON.

EDITED FROM THE ONLY KNOWN MANUSCRIPTS IN THE
BRITISH MUSEUM AND BODLEIAN LIBRARIES,

WITH AN

Introduction, a Life of the Author, and Notes,

BY

H. OSKAR SOMMER.

LONDON:
PUBLISHED FOR THE EARLY ENGLISH TEXT SOCIETY
BY KEGAN PAUL, TRENCH, TRÜBNER & CO.,
PATERNOSTER HOUSE, CHARING-CROSS ROAD.
1899

KRAUS REPRINT
Millwood, N.Y.
1990

Great Clarendon Street, Oxford OX2 6DP
United Kingdom

Oxford University Press is a department of the University of Oxford.
It furthers the University's objective of excellence in research, scholarship,
and education by publishing worldwide. Oxford is a registered trade mark of
Oxford University Press in the UK and in certain other countries

© The Early English Text Society 1899

The moral rights of the authors have been asserted

Database right Oxford University Press (maker)

First Edition published in paperback 1899

All rights reserved. No part of this publication may be reproduced,
stored in a retrieval system, or transmitted, in any form or by any means,
without the prior permission in writing of Oxford University Press,
or as expressly permitted by law, or under terms agreed with the appropriate
reprographics rights organization. Enquiries concerning reproduction
outside the scope of the above should be sent to the Rights Department,
Oxford University Press, at the address above

You must not circulate this book in any other form
and you must impose this same condition on any acquirer

Published in the United States of America by Oxford University Press
198 Madison Avenue, New York, NY 10016, United States of America

British Library Cataloguing in Publication Data
Data available

Library of Congress Cataloging in Publication Data
Data available

Extra Series, 78

ISBN 978-0-85-991735-3

CONTENTS.

	PAGE
INTRODUCTION:	
I. THE MANUSCRIPTS AND THE AUTHOR	ix
II. ANALYSIS OF THE POEM:	
α. ITS TWO PARTS	xiii
β. ANALYSIS OF THE POEM	xv
γ. THE SOURCES OF THE POEM	xx
δ. THE VERSIFICATION	xxii
ε. THE STYLE	xxii
III. THE TEXT	xxiii
THE LEGEND OF MARY MAGDALENE:	
DEDICATION (IN THE HARL. MS. ONLY)	3
PART I. HER LIFE IN SIN, AND DEATH TO SIN	9
PART II. HER LIFE IN RIGHTEOUSNESS	42
EPILOGUE IN LATIN VERSE	69
NOTES	71
INDEX OF WORDS AND SUBJECTS	77

INTRODUCTION.

I. THE MANUSCRIPTS AND THE AUTHOR.

The Life and Death of Mary Magdalene exists in two MSS. of the first quarter of the 17th century, Harleian 6211 (p. 56—94);[1] and Rawlinson 41 in the Bodleian. The latter MS. contains the author's name, "Thomas Robinson," plainly at full length; the former his initials "T. R.", and his full name blotted out, but still legible. The Rawlinson MS.[2] contains another legend of another writer, entitled *The Life of the Blessed Virgin Mary*,[3] and has the following dedication to its *Mary Magdalene*:

---

[1] A small part of the poem, altered and modernised, appeared in 1869 (February and March), in a monthly periodical called *The Westminster Abbey Magazine, or Reminiscences of Past Literature*, which lived but three months. At the beginning is a foot-note: "This poem, which now for the first time sees light of day in print, was probably written by Sir Philip Sidney—it is thoroughly Spenserian in style, and will recommend itself in a very marked manner to the poetic mind."

[2] The Curators of the Bodleian Library were good enough to send the Rawlinson Manuscript to London for me, after Mr. E. M. Thompson, the Keeper of the Manuscripts in the British Museum, had declared his readiness to take charge of it.

[3] On the cover of the volume are written the following lines, by Edw. Umfreville, who has described several of the Bodleian Manuscripts: "Mr. Robinson's *Life and Death of M. Magdalene*, I have seen and read years since in MS. It is a very pretty little thing of about 100 years old, and, I believe, never printed—its age may be found by inquiring the time when W. Taylor was fellow of Trinity College." I did enquire, but without result. The Wood Manuscript (vol. 8490, f. 172), Ashmolean Library, Oxford, which contains a list of the fellows of Trinity College, does not mention the name of Taylor at all, nor could the College library give any other information from the archives on the subject, than that a man of this name entered the College in 1670 as a commoner. The words "To the Worshippeful," etc., seem to imply that Taylor was then an old man, possibly one of the senior fellows. There is no certainty that Wood's list is complete, which would account for its omission of Taylor's name. Moreover, the dedicatory lines do not specify whether Trinity College, Oxford or Cambridge, was meant. But the list of the college of that name at Cambridge (Brit. Mus. Coll. of Cambr. and Miscell., Vol. xlv., Add. 5846, p. 230) does not mention the name of Taylor.

> "To the Worshippeful, his very kinde
> Friend, and quondam Tutor.
> Mr. W. Taylour, Bachelor of Divinity,
> and fellowe of Trin. Coll.
> T. R.
> Wisheth health, and Happinesse.
>
> When Socrates his sholars ev'ry yeare,
> Brought guifts, and presents to their Master deare,
> Among the rest 't was Æschines's device,
> To give himselfe, instead of greater price:
> My selfe (Kinde S^r) I can not nowe preesent
> To your acceptance, sith I rest ypent
> In Northern climat: but my image true,
> The offspring of my braine, I give in lieu.
> Deign but to cherrish this yong birth of mine,
> A Muse it may be, though no Muse divine.
> And thus much I with Æschines will saye,
> In commendation of my ruder lay:
> They that give much, more for themselves doe save,
> But this is all I give, and all I have.
>   Yours in all duty to
>   command
>   THOMAS ROBINSON."

The Harleian MS. has, before the Magdalene legend, a Prologue[1] in heroic couplets in the same handwriting as the sidenotes to *Mary Magdalene*. Its last ten verses are addressed to a "great Lord," who is styled the poet's grace, and who is identified by the four lines prefixed to this poem, and scrawled over with ink, but reading as follows: "To the right honourable and truly noble gentleman and Lord, Henry Clifford, Lord-Lieutenant of the midle shires of Westmoreland, Cumberland and Northumberland, T. R. wisheth all happinesse and increase of honour."[2]

At the end of this poem are the words: "Your Honours in all duty and service to commaund," and underneath, instead of a name, is a long rectangular inkblot, from which some strokes of writing

---

[1] It is of course printed below.

It begins with some reflections on the difficulties that poets have in finding a patron, and also in choosing the subjects of their compositions. The various subjects of poetry are then analysed, and some complaints made, that poetry is not so much liked and patronised as in former days, for people are rather ashamed to call themselves poets. Then follows an enumeration of many Greek, Latin, and English poets, and, finally, the profit that arises from poetry is commended.

[2] Thus the author dedicated the two different copies of his poem to different persons, as Norden did two copies of his *Description of Essex:* compare the Camden Society's print of it with the MS. in the Granville collection.

project. By using a powerful magnifying-glass, I was enabled to read, through the blot, the name "Thomas Robinson," and thus confirm the suggestion of the Harleian Catalogue.[1]

To fix the date of the MS. it was natural to inquire the time when either of the two dedicatees was living. The inquiry after W. Taylour, which Umfreville suggests, proved entirely fruitless, as I have above stated; and the result which the inquiry after Lord Clifford afforded left the matter in so far undetermined, as the Clifford family had several members of the Christian name "Henry." Mr. E. Maunde Thompson, the Keeper of the MSS. in the British Museum, was kind enough to decide the point for me, after I had myself gone wrong, by showing that the watermark of the paper on which the Legend is written is such as was used in the year 1621. Perhaps it was also used some few years earlier or later, but the difference is certainly not great, as Mr. Thompson says that the watermarks about this time change very rapidly. We may therefore reasonably date the poem "about A.D. 1621." This date falls within the lifetime of Lord Henry Clifford, the fifth and last Earl of Cumberland.[2] Moreover, the poem contains (Part II. 1132) the line,

"There stood ye Monarche of this tripple Isle," etc.,

which is internal evidence to its date, as referring to King James I., to whom this epithet was first given; for he was the first monarch who united under his sceptre the three islands of England, Ireland, and Scotland.[3]

---

[1] "The author's name at the end has been more carefully blotted out, but seems to have been 'Thomas Robinson.'"—p. 243, col. 2. The Harleian Catalogue, moreover, mentions the two poems separately, as if they had nothing to do with one another. This fact has misled the editor in the *Westminster Magazine*, so that he did not find Robinson's name, and supposed it to be written by Sir Philip Sidney.

[2] (*a*.) Sir B. Burke's *Extinct Peerage of England*, etc. (*b*.) Dugdale *English Baronage*, vol. i. p. 346: Henry, Lord Clifford, Earl of Cumberland succeeded to his father's title in 1640. He was the last Earl of Cumberland, and at his death, in 1643, this peerage became extinct, as he only left one daughter.

[3] Compare Shakspere's *Macbeth*, IV. i. 120, 121 :

"And some I see
That two-fold balls and treble sceptres carry."

This is an allusion to the union of the two islands of Great Britain and Ireland, and the three kingdoms of England, Scotland, and Ireland, which took place at the accession of James I.

Although the date was thus fixed, and the author's name attached to the poem in initials and at full length, there was little or no chance to settle the question who was this Thomas Robinson. In despite of the most careful searches through the State Papers, ecclesiastical Fasti,[1] and literary records of the time I had access to, I was entirely unable to get a satisfactory result. The name, being a very common one, occurs, it is true, several times about this date, but unless he was either the Thomas Robinson mentioned (Hardy's *Le Neve*, vol. ii. p. 186) in 1615, one of the prebendaries of St. Martin's, Lincoln, or (vol. iii. p. 637) another Th. Robinson, one of the taxors of Jesus College, Cambridge,—I know not who wrote the poem. Except one line, Part I. 25,

"Poore, silly sheapherd-swaines? ev'n such am I,"

which may be understood to mean that the poet was a minister, calling himself the shepherd of his congregation, the poem does not contain the slightest allusion to its writer. So far as we may draw a conjectural picture of an author from his work, we have to imagine a man highly educated for his time; not only well versed in Holy Scripture, but also thoroughly at home in classical literature, and a perfect master of versification. Even the name of Lord Clifford,[2] which at the first sight promises to throw some light on the author's personality, does not do so. This nobleman's life is involved in great

---

[1] I speak of the biographies and dates of divines to be got from the following works:—1. Bliss's edition of Wood's *Athen. Oxon.*, 1813. 2. Hardy's edition of Le Neve's *Fasti Ecclesiæ Anglicanæ*, 1854. 3. Dodd's *Church History of England*. 4. Tanner's *Bibliotheca Britannico-Hibernica*, 1748. 5. Bale's *De Scriptoribus Britannicis*, 1557. 6. Pit's *Scriptores illustres Britanniæ*, 1619.

[2] The following few particulars about Lord Clifford I have gleaned from, a. *Court and Time of James I.*, London, 1848; b. *The Progresses, Processions, etc. of James I.*, by John Nichols (vol. ii.), 1828; c. Gardiner's *History of England from the Accession of James I.*, etc., Lond., 1883; d. Th. D. Whitaker's *Craven*, ed. Morant, Lond., 1878. Lord Henry Clifford, the nephew of the celebrated Earl George, was made Knight of the Bath. After having married Francis, daughter of the Lord Treasurer, Earl of Salisbury, he accompanied Lord Wotton on his embassy to France. "Earl Henry," says the Countess of Pembroke (Lady Anne Clifford), "was endued with a good natural wit, was a tall and proper man, a good courtier, a brave horseman, an excellent huntsman, and had a good skill in architecture and mathematics. He was much favoured by King James and Charles I. He died of a burning fever at one of the Prebendaries' houses in York in 1643."

INTRODUCTION. I. THE MSS. AND THE AUTHOR.

obscurity, and he is but seldom mentioned in the historical records of his time. I was therefore unable to ascertain what his relations were to Thomas Robinson, or why the dedicatory inscription and the name were so carefully blotted out. Possibly the poet had changed his mind before carrying out his intention, or some unknown reasons compelled him to do so; at least his introductory lines to the *Legend of Mary Magdalene* in the Rawlinson manuscript:

> "My selfe (kinde Sir) I cannot nowe preesent,
> To your acceptance, sith I rest ypent
> In Northern climat," etc.

give rise to the supposition that he did not go voluntarily to the North. Possibly the later scrawler, I. W., who in 1682 disfigured Robinson's MS.,[1] smudged over Lord Clifford's name. I think it likely that Lord Henry Clifford never saw the poem. The lines:

> "What should I speake of those of latter yeares?
> Of Harrington among our noble Peares?
> Or of thy selfe (great Earle) the Poets grace?"

are noteworthy, because the Earl was the author of 'Poeticall Translations of some Psalmes and the Song of Solomon, with other Divine Poems.'[2] After all, the want of news about the life of the author is not so much to be lamented as one might think. If we could say this Thomas Robinson is the writer; he was born in such a year; these were the offices he held; he died when 60 years old: these few mere dates would probably make all we could hope to get about a man at this period, in which biography was not cultivated as it is now-a-days, as people were not anxious about registering all the little details of the private life of even great contemporaries.

II. THE POEM.
a. Its two Parts.

This *Life and Death of Mary Magdalene* is, so far as we know, the latest English poetical version of the life of that Saint; and it is most probably one of the last legends of Saints written in England. The late date of this legend is only intelligible from its subject. It is from its character that legendary poetry, describing the lives of

[1] See next page.
[2] See Bliss's ed. of Wood's *Athen. Oxon.* iii. 82-3, where specimens are given from the MS.—W.

Saints, martyrs, and eminent divines, developed itself always hand in hand with the ecclesiastical hierarchy. It flourished in the 12th and 13th centuries, when the Church after the Crusades had come to full supremacy over the State. From this time forward it gradually decayed, and ceased to exist when the classical revival and religious reform had shaken for ever the pillars of Church rule. But Protestantism, rooting out the worship of Saints, still acknowledged Mary Magdalene, because the Saviour himself had declared her a Saint. The poem is in eight-line stanzas, and consists of two parts, each of which has its own title. The first part: "Her Life in sin and Death to sin," comprises 107 stanzas; the second part: "Her Life in Righteousnesse," 92 stanzas. The manuscript itself is finely and neatly written, and is very legible, except in a few corrupted lines. On the margin, throughout the poem, is a concise abstract of the text, and now and then passages are cited from Holy Scripture, or from some classical writer, to which some of the stanzas refer. All the marginal notes are of a different style of writing to the text itself. In the Harleian MS. the first forty stanzas of the First Part show numerous corrections and alterations by another hand, and these are, in some cases, difficult to decipher. Sometimes only single words (especially in the rime), sometimes whole lines, and thrice whole stanzas, are altered. From the nature of these corrections, one would think that the poet himself had made them (for it is scarcely credible that any person would take the liberty to alter so arbitrarily the work of another); but their being of a far later date than the poem, proves the contrary. The original passages are much disfigured and almost effaced by the corrector. Underneath the dedicatory verses, between the words "Service to commaund" and the inkblot covering the name Thomas Robinson, almost invisible to the unaided eye, and, as it appears, wilfully effaced, Mr. Thompson found the initials I. W., and by applying a chemical re-agent to the passage he restored the number 1682. Most probably these initials and the number refer to the unknown corrector. At the end, as a kind of epilogue, are added 24 verses in Latin, headed: "De Christo cum Simone pharisaeo prandente et Mariam Magdalenam comiter excipiente." The manuscript is signed "T. R."

β. *Analysis of the Poem.*

Though the title of the poem leads us to expect a description of the facts of the life of Mary Magdalene, the work is purely allegorical, and touches but few events of real life.

After a short statement of his subject, followed by an invocation to the High Powers, that he may be kept refined and otherwise worthy of his subject, the poet plunges at once *in medias res.* The pleasurable surroundings of Mary Magdalene are described by means of a stately palace. This description (10/33) is entirely in Chaucer's style (*Knight's Tale*), and shows that the author possessed no inconsiderable amount of imagination. In this palace dwells a stately dame, gorgeously apparelled, and surrounded everywhere with all the rich treasures and stores of the known world. " Pleasure ", for this is her name (11/65), rules the loves of men, and can make happy or unhappy any of her numerous suitors whom she may deign to notice or to ignore. Her attendants are numberless. Two voluptuous ladies bear her train; " Flattery " supports her right hand; "Wantonness" her left (12/89); "Foolish Laughter" paints her eyelids, and " Idleness, Jealousy, Inconstancy, Despair, Presumption, Envy," and "a thousand other graceless graces" are ready to realize her slightest desire. She strikes her lute, and sings a sensuous song descriptive of the pleasures of the flesh, and inviting her wantons to partake of them while life lasts (13/104). Then the revels commence; and here the poet indulges in the most voluptuous and realistic descriptions (14/143). Particularly to be noticed is his fine simile, in which he compares the boundless Ocean, receiving all the rivers and casting them back again in different forms, to the ebb and flow of the various enjoyments of the hour (15/159). Among the throng of revellers is one more lovely than the rest: she is Mary Magdalene (16/191). The poet pictures her as a being supremely beautiful, and goes rather minutely into her charms, subjoining the inevitable moral regret that such a fair form should enshroud so guilty a soul, or to quote his own words, that:

" So white a wall immured such worthlesse stones " (18/245).

For the favour and love of this beautiful and angelic woman, many rivals contend; but the simile the poet brings in here, cannot be said to be particularly refined or graceful (19/263). The suitors fight together, and the successful one claims the reward of his valour (19/270). The lovers then betake themselves to a garden, which is described as containing many fair flowers, "rich and rare" (20/303). The world of Flora has been ransacked to furnish a collection of beautiful plants, such as a garden of lovers should contain (21/311), and the result is magnificent; one almost feels the fine perfume, and can feast one's eyes on the blaze of colour. Here again the poet's description suggests Chaucer (*House of Fame*). The turn of his verse is often fairly happy, such as:

> " The Damaske-roses heere were brought a bed,
> Iust opposite ye Lilie of ye Vale:
> The Rose, to see ye Lilie white, wax'd red;
> To see ye Rose so red, ye Lilie pale."

There are numerous other conceits of a similar character, which the reader will doubtless duly appreciate.

In this garden an arbour stands, where the happiness of the lovers is consummated (22/345), to their own shame and to the righteous horror of the indignant poet, who, generally ready with his moralizings, nevertheless continues his elaborate descriptions of what he seemingly deprecates (23/359). Indulging all these pleasures, and enjoying whatever can increase her sensuous cupidities, Mary Magdalene spends the best part of her life, only living for the brief hour (23/383). This opportunity the author does not let slip to " point again a moral " (24/399), although by doing so, he has not "adorned his tale."

From this life of pleasure, the Magdalene is at last aroused by the visit of a personage, whom there can be no difficulty in recognizing; it is " Conscience " (25/419). The poet describes her as possessing " myriads of eyes," having a knowledge of the future, and being the unmerciful Nemesis of every idle word and action. The advent of " Conscience " suggests to the poet an opportunity for a description of heaven with its spheres and different planets (26/439).

The workings of " Conscience " have their due effect on Mary, and she dimly begins to perceive the evil of her way (28/525). But " Pleasure " and " Custom " soon extinguish the glimmer of light, and she returns to her former estate (29/528). "Conscience" now changes her tactics, and instead of a good angel, comes again in the form of "a dreary hag of Acheron," accompanied with a "viperous brood" of torments (29/547). Mary is filled with melancholy and despair, and is hurried, and deposited with more force than elegance, before the gates of hell (31/593). The description of hell, as seen from the open gate, is, to say the least of it, original (31/599). Evidently the poet endeavoured to make it as dreadful and terrible as he possibly could, and he certainly has not failed (31/599). If making the blood curdle is a proof of art, he possesses it in abundance. Close by, sits "Melancholy" described as a man, and having a figure calculated to strike despair into the heart of Mary Magdalene (32/631). He has one peculiarity, which we hitherto imagined to have belonged entirely to the upper world; he calls for paper, pen, and ink, and wishes to indite a letter to his love (33/651). Afterwards his actions resemble those of a mad man (33/653). Mary is placed close by the side of this detestable monster, becomes his ape, and imitates his every action (33/672). Mary is thus allegorically described as being possessed of Melancholy in its most dreadful forms (34/687).

The poet then strikes out a new path, a path down a steepy way:
 "*Wrapt all in vncouth silence of the night,*" (34/696).
This second abode of punishment is as dreadful as, if not more so than, the first. Here "raging winter" and "parching summer" co-exist, and the poor wretches "frying, freeze," and "freezing, sweat" (35/723). Nemesis appears, and dispatches some of her subjects to torture Mary Magdalene exquisitely, but to spare her life (36/750). They accomplish their task thoroughly: she is led, in imagination, through deserts, over snowy tops of hills, and through populous cities, finding no rest for her troubled soul (37/783). The violent possession of melancholy and despair work on her like madness, and she fancies that she undergoes, in succession, all the fabled torments that the classic learning of the poet can bring to bear on the subject (38/823).

The first Part then closes with the description of the earth, given up to the cruel inventions of hellish thought and deed (40/863).

The second, and undoubtedly the better, Part of the poem, opens with a description of the meeting between Mary Magdalene and the Saviour (42/908). Christ is walking in the fields, which are adorned with all the flowers of May; there he meets Mary, coming down from the hills (43/915). She casts herself before him, and the evil spirits with which she is possessed, cry aloud, begging that they may not be cast out, but saved along with all those for whom he had come to die (43/925). These evil spirits, remarks the poet, know the Saviour and his mission, and thus reveal their intelligence. The Saviour is beautifully described in a paraphrase of the Song of Solomon (43/935). After that, the spirits for a second time entreat his mercy:

"*And hopinge, prayd ; but prayinge, prayd in vain*" (44/970),

but Jesus, with an awful voice, commands them to leave their habitation (45/974). His voice, says the poet, is like the thunder on Mount Sinai, which "the nations of Salem" once upon a time feared (45/977). Mary Magdalene, dispossessed of the hellish spirits, sinks down in speechless gratitude and amazement, but exhausted with the fightings of the spirits as they leave her (45/984). Christ takes her by the hand, cheers her in her tribulation, and tells her in well-known words, to go and sin no more (46/1006). Perhaps no passage of the poem shows better the poet's style of workmanship. He is nothing if not classical. In one stanza he is a Christian; in the following he has turned a thorough pagan, and Christ is styled "the winged Perseus of the Sky," and Mary Magdalene a "distressed Andromeda" (46/1007).

In a succession of figures,—such as the storm-tossed ship coming into a safe harbour, and the weary pilgrim coming to his journey's end,—Mary Magdalene is described as, at last, finding peace (46/1015). She is directed by a voice from an unseen source, to go to the courts of "Wisdom"; and there and then a dove guides her to the desired spot, much in the same way as the star did the wise men to Bethlehem (47/1033). The ways of "Wisdom"—to freely paraphrase the poet's gorgeous description of the forest through which Mary goes— are ways of pleasantness and paths of peace (47/1039). In the midst of this forest, the tower wherein "Wisdom" dwells, rears its head "to the cloudy skies" (48/1058). Certain peculiarities distinguish this tower from others; and, indeed, it is no common tower. It stands

INTRODUCTION. II. ANALYSIS OF THE POEM.   xix

on a high hill; a rock is its foundation; thorns grow before it; seas lie beyond it; deserts with wild beasts lie on either side of it, and it is protected from the curious by a "thousand toilsome labyrinths" (48/1070). Like the castles of Chaucer, Spenser, John Bunyan, and other allegorical writers, each of these peculiarities has a hidden meaning. The castle's height represents Wisdom's glories, its rocky foundation her constancy; the thorns around it, the labours which must be overcome by the searcher after Truth (48/1065). The seas, the deserts, the wild beasts, and the labyrinths are its protections against unhallowed folly.

Humility, the door-keeper, admits Mary Magdalene, who stands amazed at the glories of Wisdom's dwelling-place. As she stands, lost in wonder, Wisdom reveals herself, and is described much in the words of Solomon, for whom the poet appears to have a great fondness (49/1087). Although the words of this description are almost exactly those used in the Holy Scriptures, Robinson has wonderfully adapted them to the necessities of his stanza, betraying no small skill in versification. In this tower, within the two rooms of Wisdom, sit Solomon and David, together with "the monarch of this triple isle" (i. e. Great Britain), on whom the poet implores the destinies always to shine (50/1133). Besides these, a numerous train of attendants await her pleasure. By these surroundings, personal and otherwise, Wisdom is allegorically conceived, not as a mere abstraction, but as a real person, leading Mary Magdalene to "Repentance" (51/1148).

"Repentance" sits in a "dark closet," clad in "sack-cloth," covered with ashes, and weeping bitterly. Unseen angels minister unto her, and catch her tears as they fall, in bottles (51/1162). The poet then finds a congenial task in opposing the results of tears and repentance. First, there is one stanza devoted to tears, their uses and effects; repentance is similarly treated in the next; while a third is given up to both in alternate lines (52/1175). A certain facility of imagination is shown in these three stanzas; and some of the lines are noticeable, such as:

"Repentance, health given in a bitter pill," &c.

The Magdalene entreats "Repentance" to let her in (53/1213); and a dialogue then ensues as to why Mary seeks admission. Various reasons are given, and at last she is admitted (54/1230). By various outward signs she shows her sincere repentance, and finds to her bitter cost that

"One ounce of mirth procures a world of pains" (55/1258).

She acknowledges her former sin, and laments that she should have been made so beautiful as to cause her fall (55/1263). Some of the stanzas which record her lament are remarkably good, and worthy to be compared with the stanzas of *Mary Magdalene's Lament*, wrongly attributed to Chaucer.

With Repentance, Mary spends some time, walks forth with her, and has her for a constant companion (60/1403). Mary fancies that all nature is acquainted with her sin; and this makes her lamentations the more acute (56/1279). She grows contemplative, and sees with spiritual eyes hidden beauties in the natural objects that surround her; and this contemplation is preparative to a fuller conversion (58/1359). She gets to know that Christ is with Simon the Pharisee, and she overcomes her scruples so far as to determine to go and seek her Saviour (62/1444); but before doing so, she provides herself with the box of precious ointment (62/1448). Then the well-known biblical incident that took place in Simon's house is described (62/1451). The poet takes the opportunity given him by this incident, to indulge his taste for hidden meanings. The glory of Christ is apostrophized, and the former and latter loves of Magdalene compared (65/1530); the parable of the debtors told to Simon is brought in, and various lessons, more or less useful, are drawn from it by the poet, who particularly emphasizes the rebuke which the Pharisee received (66/1551). Mary then gets pardon for her sins, and is sent away rejoicing (66/1559); and the true nature of her repentance is shown in her subsequent good life, and her great sorrow for Christ's death (67/1583). The poem ends with the description of Mary Magdalene's meeting the risen Saviour in the garden, and her joy thereat (68/1607).

γ. *The Sources of the Poem.*

Robinson's poem proves to be entirely different from all the known earlier versions[1] of the life of Mary Magdalene, not only

[1] α. Version of the Laud Manuscript; β. Version of the Auchinleck MS.,

INTRODUCTION. II. THE SOURCES OF THE POEM. xxi

with respect to the style (which would be quite intelligible from the different date), but also in the way of treating the subject itself. The earlier versions, without exception, treat of Mary Magdalene as the daughter of Cyrus, and sister to Lazarus and Martha. They describe her falling into certain evil ways in her youth; her chastisement by being possessed of seven devils; her salvation by Christ; her sincere repentance, and the service that she rendered to the Saviour in the house of Simon the Pharisee; and they finally speak more fully about that part of her life which she spent after her conversion in attending the Saviour. Robinson, on the contrary, describes elaborately the part of her life preceding the moment of her salvation, and only outlines the other part. He does not mention anything at all of her father Cyrus, her brother Lazarus, or her sister Martha. It is a well-known fact that the early Christian writers were much exercised in discovering whether Mary of Bethany, —according to John xi. 2, xii. 3; cf. Matthew xxvi. 6,—the sister of Lazarus, and Mary Magdalene, who followed Jesus from Galilee, were identical with each other and with the penitent 'sinner' of Luke vii. And this question, so often discussed, is not yet answered, and will most likely remain unanswered, as the Holy Scriptures do not afford sufficient evidence. Whether Robinson, as a learned divine, acted purposely,—being of the opinion that Mary, sister to Lazarus, and Mary Magdalene, were different persons,—or whether he thought it better not to mention these particulars on account of the allegorical treatment of his subject, cannot be decided. His poem gives the impression, that, by describing the illustrious penitent woman whom Christ himself gave as an instance of true repentance, it was more his purpose to point a moral than to make an interesting and minute description of her life.

Some resemblance is to be noticed between the *Digby-Mystery* Mary Magdalene,[1] and Robinson's legend. (The counsel of the

---

Edinburgh. γ. Version in Bokenam's Collection. I. Band, Koelbing's Altengl. Bibliothek. δ. Version of the Barbour Collection. ε. Version of the Harl. MS. 2277 (fol. 38 *b*), going to be edited by Dr. C. Horstmann for the Early English Text Society. And finally, ζ. Version of the Harl. MS. 4196 (fol. 157). (α. β, γ, δ, ζ edited by Dr. C. Horstmann).

[1] New Shakspere Society: *Digby Mysteries*, ed. by F. J. Furnivall. 1881.

xxii   INTRODUCTION. II. VERSIFICATION AND STYLE.

devils, how to make Mary sin, and to serve them; her seduction by Lechery, and some of the allegorical personifications, are somewhat similar.) Nevertheless, this resemblance is not sufficient to give rise to the hypothesis that Robinson took the former as his source. Perhaps Robinson saw or read this play, or else knew another source of the life of Mary Magdalene which we do not possess. The accounts of her life under July 22, in the *Legenda Aurea* and the *Acta Sanctorum*, which were most likely to have been the sources, agree with the above-mentioned earlier versions, and are therefore out of the question. In my opinion, the style of treating the subject is Robinson's own original idea; his principal source for the Magdalene's life being the Gospels, and for his poetical descriptions and adornments some parts of the Holy Scriptures (especially the Song and Wisdom of Solomon), and the classical Greek and Latin writers. The marginal notes, already mentioned, cite in many cases the passages in question.

δ. *The Versification.*

The whole Poem is in iambics, the Introduction in 5-measure couplets, the Enchantress's Song (I. 105—142) in 4-measure couplets, and the Life is in Chaucer's and other writers' customary 5-measure stanza,[1] *ab abb, cc*, but with an added 6-measure line, *c*, ryming with the couplet *cc*. Robinson thus imitates Spenser in binding up his stanza with a 6-measure line, though Spenser's stanza is 9-lined, and rymes *ababb, cbcc*, as against Robinson's 8-line *ababb, ccc*, a form which Giles Fletcher the younger had earlier adopted in his "Christ's victorie and triumph in Heaven and earth, over and after death," Cambridge, 1610 : see Guest's *Hist. of Engl. Rhythms,* ed. 1883, p. 668.[2]

ε. *The Style.*

In this, as in the form, Robinson has evidently made Spenser his model, and can thus be called a Spenserian in the true sense of the

---

[1] It is often called "Rime Royal," because James I., following Chaucer, used it in his *Quhair*. The stanza occurs in Old French before Chaucer's time.

[2] On Sir Thos. More's occasional use of a final 6-measure line, see Guest, p. 669, note.

word. One spirit pervaded all Elizabethan poetry, and although Classical Literature has been at all times more or less the model for English poets, and influenced their compositions, yet it never exerted that influence so powerfully as in the 16th and the beginning of the 17th centuries. A poem in which—as in Robinson's—the ideas of Christianity are blended with the mythological conceptions of the ancient Greeks and Romans, in which allegory so entirely prevails, and which is marked by such a profusion of classical names, could only originate in a time, when the classics, brought back to a new life, were so carefully studied, and had so powerful and constructive an influence upon every branch of literature, as in the days of the classical revival and the epoch that followed it. As to the language, the poem contains comparatively few archaisms, but is peculiarly marked by many words which one recognizes at the first sight as the author's own coinages; such as "ramillets, pillastrells, turrulet," etc. Particularly to be noticed are his numerous *de* formations; such as "deglorious, depurpured, debellished," etc.

III. THE TEXT.

As to the text, the Harleian and Rawlinson manuscripts differ very little from each other, but the Rawlinson does not contain any of those alterations which are found in the Harleian. I have, therefore, as those corrections were evidently not made by the author himself, restored the passages in question by help of the Rawlinson Manuscript, and mentioned the corrections in foot-notes, where I also quote the few variations between the two manuscripts. The orthography of the MS. has been strictly preserved. The side-notes of the MS. are set in Clarendon type; those in the ordinary Roman type are by Mr. Furnivall, who added them while reading the proofs and revises of the text with the MS. during my absence in Germany.

The Harleian MS. was pointed out to me by Dr. Carl Horstmann. Both he and the authorities believed it to be unique, and neither knew anything of its author beyond his initials, T. R. A search through the Bodleian Catalogues disclosed to me Robinson's Rawlinson

MS.; and that, when it reached London, proved to be the same as the Harleian copy, save as to its Introduction and corrections. Saving Robinson's legend of M. Magdalene from oblivion, the present edition enriches the treasure of English poetry by another monument, and the list of English poets by a new name, although no particulars can be added as to its bearer. May it be useful to the student of the poetical spirit of the time, and contribute in particular to increase the knowledge of the development of the English tongue!

It is with pleasure that I express my thanks to Dr. Horstmann, and the Authorities of the Bodleian and British Museum Libraries —especially Mr. E. Maunde Thompson—for their kindness and courtesy.

OSKAR SOMMER.

London, March 13, 1884.

ERRATA (1899).

Owing to an unfortunate oversight, the *Notes* (pp. 71-76) have not been revised, and contain a number of literal errors, especially in the spelling of proper names. Besides these, the reader is requested to note the following corrections :—

P. 71, note on line 52. The writer intended is more probably Sir John Harington (1561-1612), the translator of Ariosto.

P. 72, *dele* note on line 178. (*iarre* is simply = 'jar').

P. 73, note on lines 459-461. The passage quoted is irrelevant. The reference should be ' Part. 2, lib. 6 ' (which deals with the heavenly bodies, in two chapters).

P. 74, note on lines 759-66, for *montis* read *mentis*, and for *Gebennali* read *Gehennali*.

P. 76, *dele* note on line 1574.

The Legend of Mary Magdalene,

FROM THE

HARLEIAN MANUSCRIPT 6211,

AND THE RAWLINSON MS. 41 IN THE BODLEIAN LIBRARY.

(THE DEDICATION *IS IN THE HARL. MS. ONLY.*)

H = Harleian MS. 6211.
R = Rawlinson MS. 41.

To the right honourable and truly
Noble gentleman, Lord Hen:
Clifford, Lord Liuetenent
Of the midle shires
Of Westmorland,
Cumberland, and
Northumberland
T : R : wisheth all happinesse
and encrease of honour.

Where should a Poet nowe a Patron finde,   *How can a Poet*
To please his own, and please his Patrons minnde?   *please his Patron?*
Some, Satyres; others, Epigrammes, desire;   *Men admire such*
Some, Cronicles and Warlicke strains admire;   4 *different things:*
Others, a deepe conceited Pastorall,
Or Elegiacks at a funerall :
Some are halfe rauish'd with a Tragicke style,
Others affect the gentler Comicke smile :   8
Some one perhaps (and not without desart)   *some, Hero*
Likes Heros hand and yonge Læanders heart,   *and Leander;*
Sung by diuine Musæus in a story
Of loue-sicke passion, worthy of all glory :   12
Others, an Emblem or quaint Epitaphe,   *[leaf 53, back]*
Or merry mad conceipts, to make one laugh :
Some loue diuiner poems, and in this,   *others, Divine*
Deserue to be commended; but they misse   16 *poems;*
In makinge a iudicious choyce : For why,
With painted flowers of Ethnicke Poetry,
Good matters (say they) must not be endited,
But rather in plaine easy termes recited :   20
Others, regardlesse of the Muses dity,[1]   *others, like Plato,*
With Plato banish Poets from their city,   *despise Poetry.*

      [1] Corrected by a much later hand to 'ditty.'

DEDICATION TO LORD HENRY CLIFFORD.

<table>
<tr><td></td><td>Because they are too vulgar, and no kinde
Of Poetry whats'e'r can please their minde:</td><td>24</td></tr>
<tr><td></td><td>In faire Encomiasticks to commend,
They count it flattery; to reprehend
In sharpe-fang'd Satyres, is to libellize,
To raise vile slaunders, and false infamies:</td><td>28</td></tr>
<tr><td>They condemn comedies.</td><td>Base, the Comœdian's witty mirth *they deeme*,
And Epigrammes, phantasticall *doe seeme:*
Thees are a sect, of which most men partake,
That li*t*le reckonning of the Muses make.</td><td>32</td></tr>
<tr><td>The Brazen Age has come back.</td><td>The brazen age is nowe return'd agen,
And hath defac'd the Poets siluer pen;
Whereas in former time, the greatest men
Were not asham'd to be call'd Poets then:</td><td>36</td></tr>
<tr><td>Yet of old, Poets flourished.</td><td>Witnesse Augustus, in whose Laureat time,
Learning and liberall arts were in their prime,
And Poets flourish'd: Persius (though a Knight)
Was not ashamed, Satyres to recite;</td><td>40</td></tr>
<tr><td>[leaf 54]</td><td>Propertius, borne of enobled race,
T'indite Elegies, thought it no disgrace.
And sweet Amphion, sonne to princely Ioue,
With his shrill Musicke made the stones to moue.</td><td>44</td></tr>
<tr><td></td><td>Nor did this art moue onely in their sphœre:
An Helicon hath not been wanting heere.
Then sent forth Cydney, glory of his time,</td><td></td></tr>
<tr><td>Chaucer and</td><td>And Chaucer, auld, who for his a*unt*ient rythme</td><td>48</td></tr>
</table>

29 and 30. The rime is altered thus by the corrector of H: doth seeme—they deeme.
  32. Altered by the Corrector of H. to 'little.'
  41—42. nearly blotted out.
  43—44. crossed through.
  46. *A*. Corrector. ? MS. An, or One.
  47—48. altered by H. Corrector as follows:
   Witness great Sydney, glory of his time,
   Chaucer and Spencer, who for his ancient rythme, etc.
In despite of this alteration, line 50 reads "his memory." This correction shows distinctly that he who revised the poems was quite ignorant about the date of their origin; Robertson is not likely to have seen any poetry of Spenser and Sydney. The name "Cydney", which occurs in the original passage, can only

DEDICATION TO LORD HENRY CLIFFORD.

Obtein'd a monument of lasting praise,
That kept his memory to thees our dayes.
What should I speake of those of latter yeares?
Of Harrington *among our* noble Peares?   52   Harrington won praise.
Or of thy selfe (great *Earle*) the Poets grace?
Why then should Poets be esteem'd so base?—   Why are Poets now despised
Because their pouerty o'rcloudes their witt,   because they're poor?
And makes men rather scorne, then pity it?   56
Shall vertue, which in riche men we adore,
Be e'r the worse esteemed in the poore?
Or can not some mens honours credite lend,
To that, which others meannesse doth offend?—   60
Beside, I might recount in ample wise,   Poetry profits:
The profites that from Poetry arrise.
Where each thinge, truly acted, we may see,
As in a theatre: Aratus, he   64
Shewes vs *the p[re]s[ences] of* spangled starres;
And Lucan singes the broyles of ciuill warres;   Witness Lucan,
Of loue, and louers trickes, Catullus tells:
With warlicke stratagems, *grave* Virgill swells,   68   Virgil, [leaf 54, back]
And makes his verse each circumstance betoken,
That one would thinke the matter done, not spoken.
Ovid is various, and in nimble paces,   Ovid,
The love of Gods, the flight of nymphes, he traces,   72
And well he calls it transformation,
For he [reuiues] again the [antique] fashion,

refer to Sir Henry Sydney, the father of the known poet, or to some other nobleman, who can not be identified.
    51. MS. latter. H. Corrector 'later'.
    52. altered by H. Corrector to 'and other.'
    53. Sir. H. Corrector.
    62. profitts. H. Corrector.
    65. both spheeres and poles. H. Corrector. This alteration spoils the metre. If 'presences' is the right reading of the obliterated word, it is used for the figures of the constellations which Aratus described in his chief poem.
    68. sweet. H. Corrector.
    73—4 much scribbled over by the Corrector. 'reuiues' is only a guess at the reading; 'antique' is probably right.

DEDICATION TO LORD HENRY CLIFFORD.

    Transforming truth into a witty fable,
    So to delight the mindes of the vnstable: 76
    His seas of sorrowe, holy dayes, and rites,
    Letters of passion, arte of loues delights,
    In eu'ry kinde may teach the rude some skill.
    Hesiod *giues instructions* to till;   80
Homer,   And Homers lofty style would make one doubt,
    Whether he better sung, or Hector fought.
Horace.   Martiall lends witt; Horace, in sharpe essayes,
    Against the vices of his time inveighes.   84
    Empedocles, in verses did attire
    Secrets of Nature; and the Samian Sire,
    Morall Philosophy could grauely teach.
    But Chrysostome had a farre higher reach: 88
    And wise Prudentius, with other Sages,
    Haue writt diuinely in thees latter ages.
    What should I bringe Poets antiquity?
So also Deborah,   From Deborah, and Moses victory?   92
    What should I tell of Simeon, and Mary?
and David.   Of Salomon, and Dauid, that could vary
    Musicall notes vpon his well-tun'd stringe:
    When the Angellique troopes doe praises singe,   96
[leaf 55]   And harmony, that nowe is brought to ground,
    Seemes to begin amid the sphœres so round?
    Much might I speake in praise of Poet's di*t*y,
    And make my gates farre larger then my city.   100
    I may commend, not mend them with my pen,
    For Patronage belonges to greatest men.
    And more to saye were vaine: For Poetry
    Liues of it selfe, though Poets helplesse be.   104
Be, then, my Mœcenas!   Yet some Mœcenases this age hath left vs,
    (Though of Mœcenas, time long since bereft vs,)
    That fauour learning, and accept a lay,
    Though ne'r so mean, though clad in simple grey.   108

    80. altered to 'Hesiod instructions giues us how to till.'
        99. Corrector, ditty.

DEDICATION TO LORD HENRY CLIFFORD.

Amonge the which, since chiefe I reckon thee,
Accept (great *Peare*) this ruder rapsodie.   *Accept, great Earl, my rude lines!*
And though no *Muse* I am of great desart,
Yet fauour graunt; because I loue the arte!   112
Thy better iudgement happily may spie
The slender twist of my sleight Poetry:
Yet fauourably take it in good part,
(If there want wordes, be sure there wants no heart,) 116   *They flow from my heart.*
And shine vpon my Muse with gracious rayes,
So shall it muse to sonnet out thy prayse.

        Your Honours in all duty, and
        Seruice to Commaund,

     Thomas Robinson.

110. Sir . . . rhapsodie.—H. Corrector.
111. Poet I'm.—H. Corrector.

[PART I.]

The Life and Death of Mary Magdalene,
OR,
Her Life in Sin, and Death to Sin.

1.

The death of her that was but newly borne :	1	The hypothesis or subiect of the discourse.
The birth of her that longe agoe was dead :		
The life of her, whome heauen and earth did scorne :		
Her beawty, that wast *erst*[1] debelished :		
How[2] snowy white inveild the crimson red,	5	
And yet the lily sprange vnto the rose,		
Vnder his[3] spiny fortresse to repose ;		
How sorrowe, ioye, and ioye *againe* did sorrowe close.	8	

2.

How night disrobed of her sad attire,	9	[leaf 56, back]
Put on the glitteringe *stole* of brightest day :		
How *dreary* Acheron did once retire,		
And needs would goe vnto the milky way,		
To quench his wild fire, and his heat allay :	13	
How am'rous heau'n earth, earth heau'n did viewe :		
How the ag'd Eagle did her life renewe,		
And blacke not *to be dy'd*, receiud an other hue :	16	

[1] The words in italics are those altered by some later hand in the Harleian MS. For *erst* the Corrector writes *once*. The stanzas are numbered in the MS., and lines 6, 7 of each stanza are inset, to bring-out the fact of the 8th line having 6 measures instead of 5.
[2] 'How' altered from 'Her.' [3] his—MS. altered.
   8. againe—Corrector : original blotted out.
   10. leams (or beams).—H. Corrector.
   11. pitchy.—H. Corrector.
   16. MS. altered, seemingly from 'bee dyed.'

PART I. THE PALACE OF PLEASURE DESCRIBED.

3.

<small>The authors invocation.</small>

This *bee* the dity of my oaten reed, 17
Too meane (alas !) such mysteries to tell :
Yet heauens mirrour daine mee this one meed !
In earthen vessels, heau'nly soules may dwell,
And sandy caskets oft invest the pearle : 21
 Æthereall states, and high Angellique traines,
 (Blest bee the time !) haue sometime tooke ye paines
To visit Abells sonnes, poore, silly sheapheard-swaines.

4.

<small>I pray that I</small>

Poore, silly sheapheard-swaines ! eu'n such am I : 25
(Farre bee prœsumption from an humble minde !)
I will not, (oh, I dare not,) soare too highe,
Least hee, that all enlightens, strike mee blinde :

<small>may be enabled to write of Mary.</small>

Sooth, this is all I craue, to be refind, 29·
 So to endite a laye with siluer pen,
 Of Mary, and of Marys sonne : and then
Her life, his loue declare, her loue, and life agen. 32

5.

<small>[leaf 57]
The narration of Mary Magdalenes life described by ye Palace of Pleasure, whither shee retaind.</small>

Vnder th' Appendix of a hillocke small, 33
A stately palace *in a dale* was plac't,
Fairely incircled with a marble wall,
And with a court of shininge Amber grac't.
The Chrystall windowes too, were interchast 37
 With Iacynths, Diamonds, and Sappheirs blew[e] :
 Too happy treasure for so damn'd a crewe,
That newe sins hoary make, and ould sins *aye* renewe. 40

6.

<small>Pleasure poetically</small>

The squared *greeces* were of beaten gould, 41
(Oh might it euer thus bee trod on ground !)

---

17. is.—H. Corrector. 19. heauens. ? MS.
22. ? MS. Æthercall. R. spells "Angellicke."
28. least = *lest*. 29. H. Corrector reads "truth."
34. H. Corrector, on y^e plain. 40. H. Corrector, soon.
 41. H. Corrector, steps were all.

PART I. THE GODDESS OF PLEASURE DESCRIBED.   11

Pillars of Iu'ry did the frame vphould :   described by her
Ouer the brasen gates stood Venus, crownd   Palace.
With Myrtle chaplets, in a charret round,   45
  Drawn by two siluer doues, more innocent
  Then shee her selfe : in the same continent
Blind Cupid seem'd to shoote, and tender hearts *vprent*.

7.

A turrulet tooke vp each angles shade :   49   The Palace of
Two in the middle stood, iust opposite :   Pleasure
                                               described.
The battelments of smoothest Iett were made :
A glorious out side, eu'ry where so bright,
The braine it dizieth, and dimmes the sight.   53   [leaf 57, back]
  Doubtles Alcides leaft his pillars there,
  Baccus his Elephants, and Sol his sphœre ;
While each was chear'd with ioye, and overioyd with
  cheare.   56

8.

The nimble shaddowes skippinge here a pace,   57
Seem'd in the Amber courts to sporte, and play,
Like wanton kidds vpon some steepy place,
Or tender *lambkins on* a sommers day :
So doth Apollo's euer-sparkelinge raye   61
  Daunce through the heauens spangled firmament
  To solitary earth, so male-content,
And backe from heau'n to earth, in lue of loue is sent.   64

9.

Within this palace dwells *a gentle spright*   65   Aphrodite
Soft, sweete, smooth, tender, Goddesse of all pleasure   described.

43. Pillars. H. Corrector : the original word looks like Finiales.'
45. Myrtle : first ' Mirtle.'
48. H. Corrector 'to taint.' ? MS. ' vprent '.
60. H. Corrector " lambs upon a summers ".
65. H. Corrector " A queen of loue."
66. H. Corrector cuts out 'Soft', and puts 'fair' after 'smooth' : 'sweete, smooth, faire.'

By her owne beauty, wealth, and suiters.	Amorous, younge, *faire* slender *Aphrodite*,
	To whome the Lydian wealth, the Indian treasure,
	The Falern wine is brought in lauish measure; 69
	    The Thyme of Hybla, and the Libyan flore,
	    The gemms of Tagus and the golden shore,
	With swetest odours and Assyrian Spikenard store. 72

10.

[leaf 58]
By her apparell.
 	
Aphrodite, the Goddess of Pleasure described.
	About her head a veile of lawne shee wore; 73
	Her garments were of skarlet rosy red:
	A goulden bowle in her right hand shee bore,
	Wherein all pleasure and delight were bred:
	The nations came to her *deprostrate* bed: 77
	    Happy was hee, that could obtaine a kisse;
	    Vnhappy he, that of her loue did misse:
	Yet, oh most happy misse, and most vnhappy blisse! 80

11.

By her attendants.
	Two Ladies did vphold the Damsells traine, 81
	Plumpe, pursiue Luxury, and quainter Pride;
	The one *streight* lac'd, and *boulstred in amaine;*
	The other in a gowne, large, loose and wide.
	Both, nearer then the rest, went by her side. 85
	    Easier it is to empty out the seas,
	    Then her with clothes, and her with dainties please:
	In flittinge vanities (God wot) so litle ease! 88

12.

Flattery, Wantonness.	Her right hand, guilded Flattery supported; 89 Her left, did fickle Wantonesse vpbeare; Foolish *dame* Laughter thither too resorted, To paint her eye lids, and her browe to cleare.

67. H. Corrector 'beauteous soft, slender, as a doue.'
68. Lydian: first, 'Lidyan.'
70. ? first 'Thime,' 'Libian,' 'flore': H. Corr. 'flower.'
77. H. Corrector "inuiting."
83. H. Corrector, strait—twisted was amane.
91. H. Corrector, And Foolish Laughter.

PART I. THE SONG OF THE GODDESS OF PLEASURE. 13

Idlenesse too, and Iealousy was there,   93 Idleness, &c.
   Inconstancie, Despaire, Prœsumption,
   And Enuie, that would brooke no Paragon,
Put their worst garments of, and their best faces on. 96

13.

A thowsand graceless Graces more be-side,   97 [leaf 58, back]
Attended on her, ready at her call:
They *nowe* awaited, *but* for winde and tide.
The*y* launch into the deepe, hoist sayle *and* all.
"Come (saith th' Enchauntresse) *t is our nuptiall*, 101
   Let others sad and sullen liue, while wee
   Swimme in the sweets of loue and iollity!"
So, tinklinge on her lute, shee made this harmony: 104

   "Come, come, my louers! make no stay!   The Song of the
   Let's take our pleasure, while wee may: Goddess of Pleasure.
   See, how the canopies all ope'[1]
   To entertaine our loues do hope: 108
   See howe the silken beds '*g:n* swell,
   Daringe vs their pride to quell.
   Gold and Amber in their places,   By her charme.
   Bid vs come, and see our faces: 112
   The pretty pearle lends many a smile,
   The sparklinge gemms our sight beguile,
   While the marble pillars weepe,
   'Cause wee are not yet a-sleepe.   116
   Hearke, howe the musike doth delight,
   Of that yonge slender catamite!
   See, the snowy virgins white,   She has lovely maidens,
   Hands and lipps, and heart invite.   120

[1] A later side-note in H. says 'See Proverbe Solom Har:'
      99. H. Corrector, only waited for y^e.
      100. H. Corrector, Thei ... with.
      101. H. Corrector, let vs merry be.
      102. all scribbled over by the Corrector.
104. H. Corr., Striking her Iu'ry lute.   109. H. Corr., do.
      111. their: MS. y^r.   113, 129. H. Corr., y^r.
      117, 118. scribbled over by H. Corr.

14 PART I. THE GODDESS OF PLEASURE'S PALACE.

[leaf 59]

and brave men attending on her;

and about her everything that can ravish the senses.

    Thousand Hellens faire, I haue
And as many Troians braue;
Richly they attired bee,
Onely to attend on mee. 124
What so'er the sence doth rauish,
Heere it swimes in plenty lauish :
Ioue to mee hath brought his courte,
And the Naiadës heere sporte : 128
The Dryadës their groues have left,
And haue stol'n to me by theft;
While ye Cocheman of the Sphœre
Loues to driue his horses heere : 132
Neptune too, and Thetis greene,
In my palace may bee seene.
Neuer saile out of the land!
I can giue ye*e* Tagus sand : 136
Neuer goe to *Colchos* shore!
I haue Golden fleeces store.
Shades, yee wander all in vaine;
Th' Elysian feilds are in my plaine. 140

Let all take their pleasure!

Then come, my louers, come away!
Let's take our pleasure, while wee may!" 142

14.

[leaf 59, back]

By her excesse, and company.

This said, a thowsand prostitute delights, 143
Flewe vp and downe ye courts as bright as day :
Gluttonie, to a feast her guests invites,
And Baccus, to the wine is gone his way :
Others more eager, ceaze vpon the prey : 147
  The tables richly were adorn'd with store,
  Of delicates, *not known in times of yore.*
Such, Cleopatra gaue, vnto her Paramour. 150

129. their : MS. y^r.   131. H. Corrector, Coacheman.
135. saile : first 'faile.'   136. H. Corrector, ye.
137. Colchos.—H. Corrector.   ? Original word.
148, 151, 152, 162. with. MS. wth.
149. H. Corr., which scarse were known before.

PART I. LIFE IN THE PALACE OF PLEASURE. 15

15.

The chambers were perfum'd with odours sweet, 151 Sweet chambers,
And strow'd with fragrant flowers eu'ry where.
The Damsells naked stood (ah, too vnmeet!) naked girls,
The Flute, the Lute, the *Timbrell* sounded cleare : music,
Flagons of wine were brought, to mend their cheare. 155 and wine.
  'T was hard to say, which had the most delight,
  The taste, ye touch, the hearinge, smell, or sight :
So ioye triumph'd o'r greefe, and day dispelled night.

16.

As, when ye boundlesse, brauinge Ocean, 159 Comparison.[1]
Imbezilinge ye riuers all in pride,
Receiues their waters in his ample maine ;
Some backe againe retire with curled tide,
Some through ye mountaines to ye valleys glide, 163
  Some struggle with ye brine, and foaminge flie
  Vp to the pauement of the valted skie,
And downe againe, as lowe as hell, they fall, and die ; 166

17.

So soone this crewe dispers'd : some to their sporte, 167 [leaf 60]
Some in greene arbours spent the *liue longe* day ; All the Goddess's followers disport themselves.
Some staulked round about ye amber court ;
Others to gaminge fell, and such like play,
And heere and there a drunken louer lay, 171
  Who, by his giddy, braine-sicke concubine,
  Disgorg'd ye venoun baite of raginge wine :
'T is sugar in the mouth ; but in the bowells, brine.

18.

Fast by, ye Lapithœ and Centaures sate, 175
Each largely swillinge in a full-crown'd bowle,

153. H. Corrector, Damsells half.   154. H. Corr., Viol.
155, 161. their. MS. y^e.   156. which. MS. w^{ch}.
  158. H. Corrector, o're ... dispell'd y^e.
    168. H. Corr. blistering.
      [1] 'Comparison' is in a later hand.

PART I. THE LOVELINESS OF MARY MAGDALENE.

<small>Some quarrel;</small>

Til their tongues tripp'd, and spake they knewe not what,
And speakinge made them iarre; and iarringe, scoule,
And scoulinge, tumults raise, and vproares foule: 179
   Downe goe the tables and the goblets *faire;*
   The ruddy wine, spilt on the Iu'ry *ware,*
Seemes like a fiery comet in the cleared aire. 182

19.

<small>some are turned into beasts.</small>

What should I tell of all might there be seen? 183
Some were transform'd to swine, and some to Apes,
Such was the power of the enchantinge Queen:
With Circes virge shee could commaund all shapes,
Or giue rancke poyson in a bunch of grapes; 187
   Or like Medusas snaky haire at will,
   Transforme y^e *wisest Atlas* to a hill.
Her Magicke knowledge good, but Magicke practise, ill.

20.

<small>[leaf 60, back]

Mary Magdalene describ'd to bee one amonge Pleasures retinue.</small>

Amonge ye wanton traines of Luxury, 191
That in her palaces themselues addrest,
One was more beautifull vnto ye eye,
More faire, more debonaire, then all the rest;
In colour and proportïon so blest, 195
   That, were shee but with softer sleepe alayd,
   Of virgin waxe you would suppose her made.
O Damsell faire without, but inwardely decay'd! 198

21.

<small>The beauty of her body described by the symmetry of her limmes.</small>

Her louely tresses of embellish'd haire, 199
Kist her soft necke, and shoulders iu'ry white:
The Apples of Hesperides weere there:
So Titan swifte displayes his blazinge light,
On toppe of Rhodope, with snow *bedight* 203
   Her eyes, as blacke as Iett, doe finely blaze,

---

177. their. MS. y^r.   180. H. Corrector, rare.
181. H. Corrector, fair.   189. H. Corrector, greatest Sages.
201. H. Corrector, of th'.   203. H. Corrector, so white.

PART I. MARY MAGDALENE DESCRIBED. 17

Rowlinge about, and they that in them gaze,
Looke for themselues in her, halfe lost, as in a maze. 206

22.

What should I of her arched browe relate,   207   Her brow,
Guilded with smiles, and amorous aspects;
The port of quietnesse, loues chaire of state?
Aurora hither her bright teame directs,
And all the while her higher race neglects.   211
  Her fluent tongue, with siluer is betipt;   her tongue,
  And from the caskets of her corall lippe,   and lips;
Ioue may diuine Ambrosia and Nectar sippe.   214

23.

Her ruby cheekes laid o'r the snowy white,   215   [leaf 61]
(Why may not An*tiques* erre?) were the rare frame   her cheeks,
That curious Apelles brought to light:
The litle birds *y*nchant*inge* hither came,
To picke ye ruddy grape*lets*, was their aime.   219
  Her nose, for Venus hill, I might commend;   her nose,
  But to the pearle, her teeth doe beauty lend,
While her eares pretty gemmes, with louely lookes
  contend.   222

24.

Next her *debared* brests *bewitch mine* eyes, 223 her bare breasts,
And with a Lethargy *my* sight appall;
But *by and by the selfe-wild heauy spies*
Vnto ye centre of her nauell fall,
From whence they starte, awaked at the call   227
  Of her *depurpur'd* thinges, *heere* at a stand,

    215. H. Corr. o're.   216. H. Corr. Ancients.
        218. H. Corrector, Inchantede.
    219. H. Corr. grapes was all.   219. their. MS y^r.
        222. H. Corr. do bend.
    223. H. Corr. soft snowy brests enchant ones eyes.
        224. H. Corr. y^e.
    225. H. Corr. suddenly ye eyling [? MS] heauy spies.
        226. H. Corr. And does to th'.
        228. H. Corr. plump—it makes one.
MARY MAGDALENE.   C

PART I. MARY MAGDALENE DESCRIBED.

her white hand,

Whither to viewe y̆ᵉ siluer of her hand,
And armes as streight as pine, or subtill Circes wand, 230

25.

Or rather cast a due-deuoted glaunce 231
Vpon the marble tressels vnder plac't:

her legs and feet.

But then her douelike feete themselues aduance:
On such, Dianas nymphes yᵉ game haue chast,
And the Nereïdes, with nimble hast, 235
 Trippe vp and downe, forward and backe again[e,]
 Amid yᵉ gentle murm'ringe of the maine,
Curlinge yᵉ flaggy lockes of the Neptunian plaine. 238

26.

[leaf 61, back]

Wonder it is, mee thinkes, without to see 239
So faire a face, (*aye mee*, yᵉ more her smart!)
And that her soule should so *deglorious* bee:

But her white breast covers a black heart.

A brest so white, and yet so black a heart;
Her worst the best, her best yᵉ worser parte. 243
 Can such faire hiues inclose such idle Drones?
 So white a wall *in*mure such worthlesse stones?
So beauteous a sepulchre, such rotten bones? 246

27.

A 'sepulchre,' that caue I rightly call, 247
Wherein her soule so longe imu'd hath been,
Bound with yᵉ fetters of a willinge thrall:

Yet she must be brought to God.

And yet that sepulchre must bury sin,
And for Astrœa make a shrine within: 251
 It cannot bee, but such a heauenly grace,
 In heauens quire at length must have a place:
But first the goodly corne must winnow'd bee a space. 254

  229. H. Corr. whether. 230. H. Corr. Or.
  240. H. Corr. alas. 241. H. Corr. polluted.
  243. H. Corr. Her best yᵉ worst, her worst yᵉ better part.
  245. H. Corr. immure.
  247—254 are crossed out by the H. Corrector.

PART I. MARY MAGDALENE WITH HER LOVERS. 19

28.

Amonge her riualls *iolly* nowe shee sate : 255
Each sues for loue, and loue to her affordes ;
But hee, that strongest was, the conquest gate :
No other arte prœuailes, no sugred words,
But force of armes, and dint of *steeled* swords. 259
   (Venus, the Sun still followes with her light ;
   If Titan fauor *thee*, her rayes shine bright ;
If hee but hide his head, Venus is out of sight.) 262

By the contention of her rivalls. She loves the strongest.

29.

So may you see alonge ye meadowes green, 263
Two sturdy bullockes, (hard it is to say,
Whither with loue, or furies flames more keen,)
Both this and that *infect* ye purple waye,
And make ye sanguine riuelets to play, 267
   Flie at each other swifter then the winde,
   And with y^r hornes y^r heads together binde :
The victor, Io gaines ; ye conquer'd comes behind[e.]

[leaf 62]

So two bullocks fight for Io.

30.

Great valour, sure to goe into ye feild, 271
And battell bid for Lady Aphrodite,
To whet ye sworde, and beare the trusty sheild,
To win ye fauor of some fœmale white :
'T were better for thy countries good to fight : 275
   There, if thou conquer, thou shalt conquered be ;
   If conquer'd, death thou gainst, or infamy :
Heere victorie is fame, and losse of victory. 278

Better fight for your country than a woman's love.

31.

The bloody broyles thus ended and allay'd, 279
Faire Magdalene (for so the Damsell *hight*)

Mary Magdalene

---

255. H. Corr. merry.   257. that. MS. y^t.
259. H. Corr. glittering.   261. H. Corr. her.
266. H. Corr. rush ore.   269. y^r = their.
271—278 crossed out by the H. Corrector.
    280. H. Corr. bright.

C 2

20 PART I. MARY MAGDALENE AND HER LOVER.

<blockquote>
Her louer for his labour *well ap*pay'd,
And all *aggladded* with his newe delight,
Led by y^e hand alonge y^e valleys bright: 283
   And, as they went, hee am'rous glaunces cas[t]
   Vpon her rosy cheekes and slender wast;
And nowe a kisse hee begg'd, and nowe his loue embract.
</blockquote>

walks with her Lover.

32.

<blockquote>
The glory of the pole did nothinge please him,   287
Apollos haire could not one glaunce allure,
Nor did ye fragrant-smellinge meadowes ease him,
The melody of birds could worke no cure;
So fond is loue, so dotingely dimure: 291
   The tender plants, and minerals vnseen,
   Conquer each sicknesse and disease vnclean;
But loue, by the same hand is kill'd and cur'd agen.
</blockquote>

[leaf 62, back]

He thinks of her alone;

33.

<blockquote>
His sences nowe no frame but hers receiue,   295
And in his fancy eu'ry member paint:
His minde, both sence and fancy doth bereaue,
And they againe his intellect attaint,
To thinke on nothinge but his seeminge saint: 299
   Her loue is all hee sees, or heares, or knowes,
   So the bewitchinge *oracle yt throughes*
About the *maidens* fancy, strange Deludinge showes. 302
</blockquote>

knows nothing save her love.

34.

<blockquote>
Vnto ye garden by, at length they hy'd: 303
Atlas his orchard was not halfe so rare,
Nor *Heloriz in midst of* Sommer pride:
Nor kinge Alcinous his cheifest care:
</blockquote>

They go into the garden of pleasure.

    281. H. Corr. Was called, her louer for his labour payd.
    282. H. Corr. enflamed.
    287. H. Corr. The spangling Diamonds rays could.
    301. (? MS. yt ythroughes.) H. Corr. Delphian tripod throwes.
    302. H. Corr. Preistess.
    303. H. Corr. The garden then at length by them being spy'd.
    305. H. Corr. feighn'd Elisium euen in Summers.

PART I. THE GARDEN OF PLEASURE.   21

Heere ye dead louers sprights reuiued are :   307
  Flora had empti'd heere her precious horne,
  With store ye beds of pleasure to adorne ;
No thistle heere was seen, ne pricle-armed thorne ; 310

35.

The Damaske-roses heere *were brought* a bed,   311 [leaf 63]
Iust opposite ye Lilie of y^e-Vale :   In it are Roses, Lilies,
The Rose, to see ye Lilie white, wax'd red ;
To see ye rose so red, ye Lilie pale ;
While Zephyre fann'd then with a gentler gale. 315
  The woody Primrose and the pretty Paunce,   Primroses and Daffodils,
  The Pinke, ye Daffodill and Cheuisance,
All in Perfumed sets, y^r fragrant heads aduance.   318

36.

Sweet Casia, and ye yealowe Marigould,   319 the Marigold,
That when the Sun bringes forth ye Orient daye,
Her armes, in signe of loue, loues to vnfould,
But closes when her Paramour's awaye :
The Cullumbine and Violets there play,   323 Columbine,
  With Couslips of Hierusalem so nice,
  Sweet Eglantine, and cloues of Paradise,   Eglantine,
Rare shrubs, and rarer hearbs, and beds perfum'd with
  spice.   326

37.

Narcissus too, that heart enamouringe lad,   327 and Narcissus.
Grewe by a springe (a chrystiall springe was nighe),
Whose siluer streames y^e gaudy flowers *agglad*,
Glidinge alonge, as if they faine would prie
Vnder the Veluet leaues, and by and by   331
  Into y^r watry cells againe they start,

311. H. Corr. Of—there was.   317. R. Deffodill.
318. y^r = their : the contraction is not extended, as it usually is in the Society's Texts, italics being here wanted for Corrections in the MS.
328. 'chrystiall', alterd by the writer of the MS.?, to 'crystall'.
329. H. Corr. make glad.   332. y^r = their.

22 PART I. THE ARBOUR IN THE GARDEN OF PLEASURE.

   But with a gentle pace, as loath to part,
   Leauinge y^r teares behinde, in token of y^r hearte. 334

38.

[leaf 63, back] The flower, mindefull of his former loue, 335
   Declines his head toward y^e neighbour springe :
   His sportefull shade, affection seems to mooue,
   Vnder ye fountaine water wantoninge ;
   Yet to ye banckes his tender rootes *y*clinge, 339
    The silken staulkes *'gan* tremble sore affraid,
    Least once againe Narcissus in his shade
   Should loose himselfe for loue, and in sad silence fade.

39.

Mary and her Lover go into Her arbour.

   All theese delights ye louers' eyes *aggrate*, 343
   But yet y^r appetite hath made no stay :
   Into an arbour nowe *at length they gate*,—
   This was the *hopefull* Period of y^r way ;—
   An arbour, pleasant, beautifull and gay, 347
    Incompast with triumphant baye about,
    And farther in, ye laden vines *y*sprout :
   If Baccus bee within, Apollo stands without. 350

40.

Its seats are of grass.

   The leauy pillastrells were neatly shorne ; 351
   The grassy seats, ye eyes to slumber wed ;
   The vaulted roofe, on ample *baulkes v*pborne,
   With Violets and Lilies was bespread,
   Like th' Azure skie with starres *b*esiluered ; 355
    The floore with many a flower was bedeck'd.
    The Gilly-flower, and Carnation speck'd,
   But Lady Rose, ye other with her beauty check'd. 358

339. H. Corr. do clinge.   340. H. Corr. do.
343. H. Corr. do charme.   345. H. Corr. they arme in arme.
   346. H. Corr. Together walke.
349. H. Corr. do sprout.   353. H. Corr. pillars borne.
   355. H. Corr. all siluered.
356. H. Corr. The fragrant seat with flowers was bedect.

PART I. MARY AND HER LOVER IN THE ARBOUR. 23

41.

On flowry beds ye Louers heere repose ; 359 [leaf 64]
And nowe sweet words must guild their bad intent : Mary and her Lover
With smiles, with lookes, with lippe and hand hee woes:
Such were ye Dartes, yt subtill Cupid lent,
Lustes wandringe harbinger, vaine complement : 363
   Faire ramillets and posies hee præpares,
   With sonnets smooth, and garlands for her haires ;
And so with gentle pace, into her brest hee fares. 366

42.

What should I tell of those polluted acts 367   do deeds of lust in the Arbour,
That followe wantonnesse and Luxury ?
Let modesty not meddle with yr facts,
Sith tongue and hart, in mischeife still agree,
And as ye wordes, ye actions often bee : 371
   Their descants nowe they tooke, and restles rest,
   And thought they were with ioyes of heauen blest ;
But night as blacke as hell, yr meltinge soules possest.

43.

The Sun peep'd in with his declininge raye, 375
And dy'd his paler cheekes with fiery hue ;
It seems, hee blush'd, and would recall ye day,   and make the Sun blush.
The wickednesse of *Vestaes sonnes* to viewe,
That rush to folly, but yr folly rue : 379
   And thou, my Muse, packe hence with nimble flight !
   The shame of sinners, 't is no great delight,
For modest eare to heare, or chaster pen to write. 382

44.

Thus Magdalene in Pleasures wanton courts, 383 [leaf 64, back]
Parte of her youthfull dayes did fondly waste,

   360. their. MS yr.
   366. H. Corr. And on her brest he slumbers, too too freed from cares.   369. y{r} facts = their deeds, doings.
   370. H. Corr. for.   378. H. Corr. Mortall men.

24   PART I. MARY WASTES HER DAYS IN VANITY.

<small>Mary Magdalene spends her time in dress and feasts.</small>

Ioyinge in vanity and idle sportes,
To spend the time, y^t soone (*God wot*) was past.
Prœuentinge all her pleasure with her haste :   387
 Parte of her time in idle languishement,
 Parte in attire, and gaudy ornament,
And parte in frolicke feasts and banquetinge, shee spent.

45.

<small>She walks;</small>
<small>she lies in bed;</small>

Sometimes the palace walkes delight her minde ;   391
Sometimes in silken beds shee *sweltred* lies ;
And nowe shee's vacant to her louers kinde,
And nowe the garden doth inuite her eyes ;
But by and by, her arbour greene shee spies :   395

<small>she bathes.</small>

 Nowe in ye springe shee bathes, to coole her heat,
 And waues her *plume*, to fanne away ye sweat ;
And cooler nowe, shee makes a sunny bancke her seat.

46.

<small>So do our fondlings wanton in their youth,</small>

So *doe* the fondlinges of our latter age,   399
In iollity their fresher yeares *d*ispend,
Treadinge this scœne, as 't were a silken stage,
But neuer dreaminge of a Tragicke end :
Can great Iehouah take him for his friend,   403
 That in his youth doth nought but wantonize,

<small>and offer only their age to God.</small>

 But when ould age decayes, both eares and eyes,
Then to ye altar bringes his haltinge sacrifice ?   406

47.

<small>[leaf 65]</small>

Let none on Magdalens delaye prœsume,   407
Though (sooth to say) it was not very longe :

<small>Yet life is but a fading flower.</small>

Life 's but a fadinge flower, a subtile fume,
A shadowe vaine, a shorte, though pleasant songe.
Then oyle your lampes betimes! and in ye thronge 411
Of Saintlie Heroes, *enter heau'n* amaine ;

<small>386. H. Corr. which (ah, too soon).   387. her : first 'his.'
392. H. Corr. softer.   397. H. Corr. Or—Fann.
399. H. Corr. euen so.   400. H. Corr. do spend.
412. H. Corr. Saintlike . . run ye course.</small>

PART I. SYNEIDE OR CONSCIENCE DESCRIBED.

For what the Fates decree, is not in vain[e :]
Ioye heere, shall sorrowe there ; teares heere, ioy there
    obtaine.   414

48.

When heau'ns bright eye, farre brighter then the Sun,
Beheld th' asp[i]ringe tower of vaine delight,
And howe this harlot had her selfe vndon,
Hee sent Syneide, daughter of the light,   *The touch of a good conscience*
To tell the Caytiffe of her wretched plight :   419 *comes from heau'n.*
    The Damsell brighter then ye brightest glasse,
    The *Isicles* in splendor did surpasse,
And in her siluer hand, a poynted *goad* there was ; 422

49.

A tiffany shee wore about her head,   423
Hanginge submissely to her shoulders white ;
From top to toe, she was immantoled   *A good con-*
With purest Lawne ; and, for her nimble sight,   *science describ'd.*
Lynceus his eyes were neuer halfe so bright :   427 [leaf 65, back]
    The Eagles quickenesse in respect is blinde,
    And Argus with his hundred eomes behinde,
For myriads of eyes about her body shin'd.   430

50.

Thinges past were prœsent to her searchinge viewe, 431
And future reprœsented in her thought,
Where newe thinges n'er wax'd ould, but oulder newe.
Each idle word and action hither brought,   *Conscience judges*
Receiue y^r doome and censure (as they ought).   435 *every idle word.*
    Sometimes in Paradise shee likes to dwell,
    Sometimes shee diues into the deepes of Hell ;
Shee sees the heart, and pries into his closest cell. 438

---

413. H. Corr. Before you set, for.
421. H. Corr. Iasper stone.   422. H. Corr. spear.
428 is : first 'was'.   435. y^r = their.

51.

Ezek: 1:	*Faine* of her message, nowe shee tooke her flight 439
Reuel: 4:	Through the bright amber of y^e flaminge Court,
The heau'n of heauens.	Passinge y^e wheeles of purest Chrysolite,
	Drawn by y^e fiery beasts y^t there resort,

Where millions of Angells euer sporte, 443
 And glorious martyrs, after all y^r woes,
 Singe praise to him y^t ouercame y^r foes,
And all ye Saints, y^r crownes, at Glories throne depose.

52.

[leaf 66] The Crystall heaven.	Then by ye Chrystall waye shee nimbly past, 447
	Vnto ye radiant spangled firmament,
	Where heauens euer-wakinge sheapheard fast,
	His starry flockes into y^r fouldes had pent.
The eighth sphœre.	The Gnossian Crowne among ye rest was sent, 451

 The Goblet, Helen, and the Brothers twaine,
 Cassiope, ye Pleiads, and ye Swaine
That Arctos kept in warde, with all ye starry traine. 454

53.

The Planets.	*And* through ye wandring sphœres shee wandringe went,
Amo: 9: 6:	Leauinge ye rasters of the starry light;
	Then to ye pure æthereall element
Zanch: de operi: Dei: Lib: 2: cap. 6:	That's whirld about ye hornes of Cynthia bright,
	Both they and shee out-strippe ye feeble sight, 459

 So rare and subtill substances they been.
 Natures so much depur'd, that (well I ween)
No mortall eye, sphœres, fire, or conscience, e'r hath seen.

54.

The ayre.	So passinge through ye tripple-region'd ayre, 463
	Where diuerse mixtures and aspects appeare:
Arist: 1: meteor:	The flyinge Dragon, ye resplendent Haire,
	The Darte, the Candle and ye burninge Speare,

---

439. H. Corr. Glad.
440. sidenote; 1st Chapter of Ezekiel, and 4th of Revelation.
455. H. Corr. Next.   455—462 crossed-through in H.

PART I. CONSCIENCE SPEAKS TO MARY MAGDALENE. 27

The Milke, the Kidds that skipped here and there, 467
   The poynted Beame, th' infatuating Fire,   Senec: lib: 7:
   The Northern Comœts and ye painted Ire,   not: quæst: cap: 5
With many more, whereof some fall, and some aspire.

55.

At length shee touch'd ye toppe of hillockes highe, 471   [leaf 66, back]
That ouer-shaddowe Aphrodites towers,
And streight-way, in ye twinkling of an eye,   Conscience winds
Shee windes her selfe into ye secret bowers   herself into Mary's heart,
Of Mary Magdalenes depraued powers :   475
   With gentle hand shee prickes her festerd hart;
   The boylinge blood from eu'ry veine '*gan* start,
And thus ye wanton mayde assaults with mickle smart :

56.

" Ah, fondling ! whither, whither do'st thou flie   479
With guilded winges of selfe opinion vaine?
Can ought escape heauens all-seeinge eye?   and asks her how
Or shall thy pleasure breed no after-paine?   she can escape God's eye.
If so, a Paradise on earth were gaine !   483
   But when ye reuolution of yeares
   Shall bee at hand, then ioy must end in teares,
And pleasant spectacles bee chang'd to ghastely feares.

57.

" Sion was holy to the Lord of yore ;   487
Salem's in-habitants his cheife delight ;
Each to his altar, freewill of-fringes bore,
And payd ye Leuite aye the Leuites right ;
So did ye temple shine with glory bright ;   491
   Religion ruld ye royall politie
   With iustice, temperance and æquitie :   She knows she
Then let not Magdalene her natiue soile denie.   494   once was pure.

58.

" Wilt thou in riot swimme, while others fast?   495   [leaf 67]
Wilt thou bee sporting, when as others pray?

    473. an : first 'a'.   477. H. Corr. doth.

28   PART I. CONSCIENCE PIERCES MARY'S GUILTY HEART.

Conscience appeals to Mary

Or canst thou still delight to bee imbrac't,
When others, drown'd in sorrowe all yᵉ day,
With sacke-cloth gird yʳ loynes, and sad araye ?   499
    Or while the aged sire 's besprinkeled
    With dust and ashes on his siluer head,
Canst thou thy various Iunonian plumes dispread ? 502

59.

"Doubtlesse those haires for lust were not intended ; 503
Those eyes for Cupids darts were neuer meant ;
That heaunly face, by art but litle mended,
(Sith nature in it all her skill hath spent,)
Was not to bee a wanton's ornament ;   507
    Those eyes were made so bright, the heauns to see ;

to be good to God.

    Those feet, to tread yᵉ paths of æquitie :
Bee not so bad to him, yᵗ is so good to the !"   510

60.

This sayd, shee brandishes her quiueringe darte,   511

She pierces Mary's breast.

And makes a deeper wound in Maries brest :
The silly soule amaz'd, beginnes to starte,
As one awaked from his nightly rest,
With slumber soft, and hopefull dreames possest.   515
    For pleasure is a dreame of sweet delight,
    That lastes no longer then yᵉ shortest night,
But when the day appeares, awaye it takes his flight ;

61.

[leaf 67, back] Or as yᵉ nimble doe in lawny parke,   519
Browsinge vpon yᵉ palate-pleasinge brier,
Is on a suddaine made yᵉ hunter's marke,
And wounded in her brest, perceiues a fire,
So Magdalene, in midst of her desire,   523
    Crown'd with yᵉ blisse of fooles, and pleasures vaine,
    Feeles in her heart yᵉ stinge of gripinge paine ;

Mary sorrows.

And then to feigne sad sighes, and sorrowe, shee is faine.

62.

But sorrowe soone in streames of pleasure's drownd, 527   *Pleasure and customa in sin choake a good conscience.*
And conscïence away doth vanish quite;
So litle truth in womens teares are found.
The Crocodile can sorrowe to yᵉ sight,
And vnder sighes embaite his venom'd spight.   531
   Vaine woman! see! yᵉ hart hath quickely found
   A saluing ditany, to heale his wound:
And shall thy heart vnsounded, still remaine vnsound?

63.

But custome is a tyrant, and his slaues   535
Are forc'd within his limits to abide.
Tis easier to still yᵉ swellinge Waues,
And turne yᵉ torrent of yᵉ strongest tide,
Then to resist his course, or quell his pride: 539
   So Mary to her lust againe returnes,   *Mary returns to her lust.*
   And at Ambrosian mercy, offerd, spurnes,
Till Heauens awefull power in zealous anger burnes.   542

64.

Withat a dreary hagge of Acheron,   543   [leaf 68]
Arm'd with a gastely torch, new dipt in blood,   *The state of a tormentinge conscience poetically describ'd.*
A sable weed, as blacke as night, put on,
And in the palaces of Pleasure stood,
Shakinge yᵉ frie of her vipereous brood: 547
   Fury attends her, and the want of sence,   *Ovid metamorph: Lib; 4; fab: 9:*
   Sorrow, Despight, with yᵉ sad Influence,
Famine, and bloody Warre, and meagre Pestilence.   550

65.

The pillars trembled at this ghastely sight;   551
The dores were tainted with a pallid hue;
The Sun, amaz'd, deny'd his wonted light,
While yᵉ poore mayd, disquieted anewe,   *Mary is disquieted.*
Striues to go forth of dores; but there a crewe   555
   Of hideous glowinge snakes yᵉ entraunce keepe,

      543. withat = 'With that'.

PART I. MARY IS TORMENTED BY HER CONSCIENCE.

That all about y̆ᵉ direfull fury creepe,
And in whole troopes from out her shaggy cauerne peepe.

66.

The snakes of Conscience twine round Mary.

Some wandred vp and downe her dismall brest; 559
Some to her pitchy armes and shoulders clunge,
With fiery eyes and hissinge tongues possest;
And one vpon yᵉ wretched mayd shee slunge,

Virgil: Ænei: 7: That twininge here and there, about her sprunge, 563
And glided on her brest with gentle hast,
And there vipereous cogitations plac't,
With pininge greife and sorrowes, yᵗ yᵉ spirites wast. 566

67.

[leaf 68, back]

The crinkled snake about her Crystall necke, 567
Seem'd like a wreathed chaine of brightest gould,
And for a fillet seru'd, her haire to decke,
For through each parte yᵉ slippery pilgrim rould,
And fire within yᵉ marrowe did infould, 571
Taintinge yᵉ sences with his poysond gall,
That soone yᵉ Damsells riot could appall,
And Sorrowe much aggladd at Pleasures funerall. 574

68.

She cannot smile. Nowe all yee flittinge daughters of the light, 575
Packe hence with speed, and see, yee bee not seene!
Let neuer smile or laughter come in sight!
For ioye and ioyllity too longe haue been

Sorrow is queen of her, Within these courtes: but Sorrowe now is queen. 579
Mary hath cast her louers out of minde,
And solace in her brest no place can finde,

and carking Care. For carking care doth all delights together binde. 582

69.

The Fury nowe (it seemes) has stood her freind, 583
And counsell'd her to bidd vaine sports adieu.
But ther 's much difference 't-wixt freind and fiend,

PART I. MARY IN THE DWELLING OF MELANCHOLY.   31

And hee, y^t monster-headed Gorgon slewe,
Did but ye ould one in younge snakes renewe :   587
   The blood, y^t Perseus heere and there did spill,
   Begate another brood of serpents still.
If Hell be cause of good, that good is nought but ill. 590

70.

Into ye hollowe of a darke-some cell,   591   [leaf 69]
The Messenger of Night conueigh'd her streight :   *The stinge of a bad conscience*
Shee thought, shee had been wafted quicke to hell,   *leads to extreme Melancholy, or*
So swift shee flewe, y^t now shee felt no weight,   *kinde of despaire.*
Till downe shee squats before a balefull gate   595
   That euer open stood, both daye and night,   *Melancholy*
   To entertaine each sad, disastrous spright,   *described by his dwellinge.*
With horrid shapes, and apparitions for his sight. 598

71.

So gape the gloomy courts of Pluto fell,   599   *It is like Hell,*
Exhalinge cloudy mistes of sulphur blewe,
With horrid damps, and many a noysom smell,
Ready to swallowe vp ye damned crewe,
That thither hast, and yet y^r hast they rue ;   603
   When death a punishment for life they se[e,]
   And life for death a punishment to bee,
And death with life, and life with death ioyne amity ;

72.

Or as ye iawes of Scyllas barkinge hounds,   607
That aye for greedinesse of booties raue,
And swallowe all that come within y^r bounds :
Such was ye gap of Melancholies caue,   *this cave of Melancholy.*
Where many loose, but fewe y^r lives can saue ;   611
   Onely for barkinge hounds, y^e grimme-fac'd cat,
   The slowe pac'd asse was there, y^e flutteringe bat,
The croakinge rauen on a slaughtred carcasse sate. 614

   593. R. whafted.   595. R. quats.   603. y^r = their.

73.

[leaf 69, back]
The ground, no whole-some hearbe, no flower breeds, 615
No fruitfull tree aray'd with sommers hue,

Foul weeds fill it.
But cóckell, darnell, thornes, and stinkinge weeds,
And wither'd trunkes, deuoy'd of leaues, in liewe
Of better plants, with y^e fauereous yewe, 619

Plin: lib: 16: cap: 26:
    Beside ye fatal tree, where Phyllis faire
    Hunge by ye tresses of her goulden haire,
For loue of him, y^t of her loue tooke litle care. 622

74.

The murdered lie there.
Heere Pyramus and Thysbe murdred lie; 623
Heere Antony and Cleopatra been;
Heere Aiax, with his bloody speare fast by;
Heere Cato, and ye Carthagenian Queen:
Sad spectacles! no sadder euer seen! 627
    Ægeus was heere, deluded once by fame;
    Empedocles leapt hither through ye flame
Of Ætna; and ye Stagirite by water came. 630

75.

[Melancholy described]
By his gesture.
But loe, within, dull Melancholy sits, 631
Proppinge with weary hand his heauy head,
And lowringe on ye ground in franticke fits,

Melancholy looks like Death.
With pallid hue hee look'd, as hee were dead,
Or Death himselfe: for many hee had sped 635

By the severall parts of his body.
    And sent vnto ye graue: rough was his haire,
    His hollowe eyes, Hyæna-like did staire,
Sparkelinge like fishes scales amid y^e cloudy aire. 638

76.

[leaf 70]
Longe eares, blacke lippes, teeth yeallowe, meagr[e] face,
Sharpe nose, thin cheekes, chin pendant, vaulted cragge,
Lean ribbes, bare loynes, lanke belly, snale-like pace,

By his apparell.
Lame feet, dead hands, and all his garments sag[ge:]

[y^r = ther]
Heere hanges a patch, and ther a tatter'd ragge: 643.
    Such Melancholy hight; and seated so,

A thousand Gorgons doe his fancy woe,
And horrid apparitions about him throughe.   646

77.

Sometimes with loue his cogitation swells,   647
And then 'gainst churlish riualdry hee braules,
And of his Ladies cruelty hee tells, *Melancholy*
And makes sad plaint vnto ye ruthlesse walles: *complains his Lady's cruelty.*
In hast, for paper, pen, and inke, hee calles,   651
   A letter to his loue hee will endite,
And with a thorne on ground hee 'gins to wright;
Then vp hee takes ye dust, and blowes it out of sight.

78.

Sometimes about ye starres his minde doth roue,   655
And light Ambition in his brest beares swaye;
And then hee will contend with mighty Ioue, *Diuerse kinds of*
And haue commaund o'r vassal Titan's raye: *Melancholy despribed.*
But, by and by, hee softely steales awaye,   659
   And slinkes from out his den, supposinge ther[e]
   Some furious hagge would him in peeces teare,
So closely couch'd hee lies, all quiueringe for feare.   662

79.

Nowe out hee hollowes, and full loudely yells,   663 [leaf 70, back].
As if hee chas'd before him some wilde beast:
But that deuise another thought expells;
And till hee finde his goulden interest,
Hid vnder ground, with feare hee is possest: 667
   Nowe hee supposes, hee's a man of glasse;
   And nowe straunge colours seeme before him passe;
And now hee thinkes, hee is not, what but nowe hee was.

80.

Hard by his side, sad Magdalene was plac't,   671 *Mary is with Melancholy in his cave.*
Within ye vgly caue of this dull spright.
Kindely each other at ye first embrac't,
But soone shee felt ye rancor of his spight,

Mary's pleasure is changed to sadness.	For all her daye was turned into night :	675
	And shee, y^t was with pleasure lately crown'd,	
	Now hanges ye head, and viewes ye cursed ground,	
	Bearinge about her still an euer-smarting wound.	678

81.

As in the splendor of a glassy sphere, 679
What s'euer hee y^t vewes it, doth assaye,
Bee sure to see it reprœsented there,
The mimicke orbe each action will bewraye,
And in a nimble shaddowe soone displaye 683
   The motion of ye foot, ye hand, ye eye,
   The lippes, ye tongue, and tell what is awry,—
Whither hee sad his browe, or looke more cheerfully,—

82.

[leaf 71]

She shares all Melancholy's fancies.

So Magdalene is Melancholies Ape, 687
And, what soe'r hee does, assayes to doe :
His fancy bringes him each fantasticke shape,
And so fantasticke is her fancy too :
Hee stayes, shee stands : hee stirres, and shee doth goe :
   Hee trembles at ye trembling of the winde ;
   Shee feares each blast : hee beares a guilty mind ;
A guilty conscience shee within her brest can finde. 694

83.

Ovid: metamorph: lib: 4: fab: 10:

There is a path adown a steepy waye, 695
Wrapt all in vncouth silence of the night,
Where wandringe (cursed hap !) poore pilgrims stray[e,]
A path, y^t leades vnto y^e lake Cocyte,

A description of Hell

Where hellish torments wretched soules affright, 699
Where deadly scritch-owles direfull dities sing[e,]

[y^r = their]

   The grisly ghostes y^r sorrowe ecchoinge,
And all about y^e aire y^e poyson'd vapours clinge. 702

84.

A thousand gates and entraunces there bee, 703
To Lethes burninge waues and scaldinge fire,

PART I. A DESCRIPTION OF HELL.   35

But backe againe, wee no returne can see;
The Lions den lets fewe or none retire:
And though ye intricate Dædalean gyre 707 Entrance is easy
  Haue many portalls, easy to attaine, to it;
Yet hee y^t knowes how to returne againe. return impossible.
May count ye countles sands, and make ye mountains
    plaine. 710
            85.

As Amphitrite in her larger wombe 711 [leaf 71, back]
Receiues all other floods and Chrystall brookes,
So doth this lake all hopelesse soules in-tombe,
And still it hath more roome, for more it lookes:
So many windinges there, and wandringe nookes, 715
  That, though all nations of ye world should cease,
  And fall together in a close-throng'd prease,
Yet boundlesse hell could ne'r perceiue his owne
    encrease. 718
            86.

There raginge winter euer doth abide, 719 Eternal cold is
And yet no showre, y^r burninge tongues to wet: there,
They allwayes haue ye parchinge sommer tide, and parching
And yet no sun, y^r frozen limmes to heat: heat,
So doe they fryinge freeze, and freezinge sweat: 723
  And (y^t which to y^r gripinge paine and greife
  Still addes a newe supplie without releife) and everlasting
Æternity amonge y^r torments is ye cheefe. 726 torments.

            87.

Hither came Nemesis, and left ye skie; 727 Nemesis
(In iust reuenge shee tooke so much delight:) Κατ' ἀνθρωπο:
Soone as shee entred with her maiesty, πάθειαν.
The ghostes inuegled with perpetuall night, enters Hell.
Stood all amaz'd, and trembled at the sight: 731
  Their eyes were dazled with her bright attire,
  But, o, they quaked at her awfull ire,
Freezinge with fearefull could amid the flames of fire. 734

                                            D 2

88.

[leaf 72]
Nemesis calls up
7 fiery Spirits,

Amonge ye blacker sonnes of Tartary, 735
Seu'n hideous fiery sprights shee euocates :
They came with speed ; yet durst not come too nigh,
Least, happily adiudged by ye Fates,
They should augment y^r chaines and heauy weights :
   For Iustice could not Stygian vassals brooke ;
   But terrified them with her angry looke,
And heau'nly maiesty in hell vpon her tooke. 742

89.

In thunder then shee spake, great silence made, 743
(At eu'ry worde shee shak'd ye gates of hell)
" Goe to ye earth, and seeke ye wanton maide
That erst in idle Pleasures courts did dwell,

Melancholy a fit
præparatiue to
possession.
and bids them
torment Mary.

But nowe remaines in Melancholies cell ! 747
   Torment and vexe her ! take away her rest !
   Enter her thoughts ! fully possesse her brest !
But spare her life ! in y^t yee haue no interest." 750

90.

So hauinge giu'n her charge, awaye shee flinges 751
From out ye cauernes of aye-lastinge woe,

Then Nemesis
goes back to the
sky.

And postes vnto ye skie with nimble winges,
Where Iris by ye waye salutes her lowe,
And on her weeds sweete water shee would throughe :
   But ye immortall power gaue no consent :
   For though vnto ye poyson'd lake shee went,
Vncapable shee was of ye sulphurean sent. 758

91.

[leaf 72, back]

The Hierarchies and Dominations bright, 759
Burned in fiery zeale and zealous fire,
Soone as thees tidings shee had tould arright,
And all with her in iust reuenge conspire :

Zanch: lib: 4:
cap: 19:

The hellish fiends were glad at Heauens ire ; 763
   And though about them they y^r to[r]ments bore,

Yet nowe more ioyfull then they were before, *The 7 damned Spirits find*
The damned spirits scund'd alonge yᵉ Stygian shore.

92.

Through sad Cimmerian[1] mistes as blacke as night, 767 [¹ MS. Cimmeriam]
At length to fresher aire they did aspire;
Though dazled with yᵉ glimmeringe of the light,
They easily found out this aged Sire : *Melancholy,*
Swift was yʳ speed, but swifter yʳ desire, 771
  Had not they been with iron chaines confin'd,
  By him yᵗ greeat Leuiathan can binde.
Then let not silly Saints bee troubled in yʳ minde. 774

93.

Soone as into his cell they entraunce made, 775
(And soone they entraunce made into his cell,)
Leauinge yᵉ borders of the airy glade,
Within yᵉ Damsells brest they come to dwell, *and take up their abode in Mary's breast.*
And thither bringe they mischeefes store from hell :
  Scorpions, and flames of Ætna, to affright;
  Madnesse and feare, with many a ghastely sight, 781
And malice (what more deadly?) like a womans spight. *Iunonis odium.*

94.

But then yᵉ haplesse maide (vnhappy tide!) 783 [leaf 73]
Incited by yᵉ monsters huge[2] within, *Virgil: Æneï: 7: et: Hom: Il: ξ:*
Runs maddinge vp and downe yᵉ citie wide,
Like to yᵉ top, yᵗ in his gyre doth spin,
When game-some lads with limber stroakes begin 787 *They drive her*
  To scourg it round about some larger court,
  That fecches compasse, while yᵉ simple sorte
Stand wondringe at yᵉ swiftenesse of yᵉ boxen sport. 790

95.

The stroakes adde heart, and driue it forward well : 791
No slower pace yᵉ maide is forcd to hie,
Through th' midst of cities, and of people fell; *through cities and woods.*
Beside, [i]nto yᵉ woods shee seemes to flie,

² MS. 'monsters hunge', with (?) n of *hunge* crossed out.

PART I. MARY IS DRIVEN ABOUT BY HELLISH SPIRITS.

  Like to ye Menades y^t 'Euhœ' crie,   795
   And in the honour of ye God of wine,
   Nourish y^r sacred haire, and doe entwine
  Their tender Iuy iauelins with ye braunchinge vine, 798

96.

  That girt about with ye faire spoyle of hindes,   799
   Their merry orgialls and iollities
   Aye celebrate, with mad outragious mindes,
  And fill ye great circumference of ye skies
  With hideous shouts, and vaste redoubled cries.   803

Mary wanders about, with hair dishevelled.

   So doth ye Damsell wander heere and there,
   Trailinge along her lowe dissheueld haire,
  With fearefull fire enflam'd, and could with fiery feare.

97.

[leaf 73, back]

  Nowe through ye aire with nimble pace shee braues, 807
   And on ye top of snowy hills is plac't;
   And nowe vnto ye dales beneath shee waues,
  And yet shee knowes no reason of her hast:

She makes her nest in deserts.

  Sometimes shee makes her nest in deserts waste,   811
   And groaues become her den, with trees around;
   But litle it auailes to hide a wound:
  A guilty conscience maye in darkest night bee found. 814

98.

  Nowe shee is catchinge Cynthia by ye horne,   815

Her fancy is disordered.

   (For so ye troubled fancy will suppose,)
   And nowe ye wandringe plancets shee doth scorne;
  Vnto ye higher Cynosure shee goes;
  But by and by a newe delusion throughes   819
   Her pride as lowe as Phlegetonticke maine.
   So litle blisse eu'n in our dreames wee gaine;
  And for such momentary ioye, such endlesse paine. 822

99.

  Heere a longe time musinge in mind shee stayes,   823
   Conceitinge shee in Pluto's court remaines:

PART I. HER TORTURES BY THE SEVEN SPIRITS OF HELL. 39

Heere flames shee sees: 'greater, my flames!' shee sayes;
There ice congeald ; but coulder are her veins ;
And all ye fictions of infernall paynes, 827   *She thinks she*
    Shee to her selfe ascribes : dire vulturs rent   *suffers all the pains of Hell,*
    Her bowells, Tityus-like ; and shee is spent
With longing for ye fount and tree neare-imminent. 830

100.

And Sisyphus his stone, shee makes account, 831   *[leaf 74]*
Comes rouling, troulinge downe ye hill againe,   *with Sisyphus,*
That erst shee labour'd vp ye steepy mount :
And nowe shee must endure Ixions paine   *with Ixion,*
On ye tormentinge wheele : then all in vaine 835
    With Danaus his daughters shee helpes fill   *and the daughters*
    The siue-like vessells, y^t ye water spill   *of Danaus.*
Out at a thousand holes, y^r taske renewinge still. 838

101.

Thus (ah poore soule !) shee 's tossed too and fro : 839
The deadly feinds, y^r furious will obtaine :   *The violence of*
And nowe her body headlonge downe they throughe,   *possession.*
Into ye brinish waters of ye maine ;
And nowe in fiery flames shee 's allmost slaine : 843
    Sometimes shee liues in dens and hollowe caues,
    Sometimes shee has her dwellinge in ye graues,
And sometimes on ye top of ragged rockes shee raues.

102.

No freinds can now persuade her to abide ; 847
No bolts of iron can her feet detaine :
The spirits driue her on with winde and tide :   *She is driven*
(Where reason's failinge freindshippe is but vaine)   *about,*
Fetters, like limber strawes, shee breakes in twaine, 851
    And then vnto ye monuments shee flies,
    Where, groavelinge on the ground, shee breathlesse   *and falls down.*
       lies :
When (poore distressed soule !) oh when, wilt thou
       arrise ? 854

103.

[leaf 74, back]

Vnhappy seruants to such Fairy nymphes! 855
Vnhappy younglinges, that haue such a sire!
Vnhappy handmaides to such cursed impes,
That, for a litle sweete of vaine desire,
Adde paine to paine, and fuell to ye fire! 859

The writer pities Mary.

Vnhappy Magdalene! vnhappy I!
Vnhappy all vnder ye azure skie,
Had not heau'n pity'd earth, and life been pleas'd to die. 862

104.

No cruelty is as bad as Hell's.

No cruelty with Hellish, maye compare, 863
For, from this fount, all cruelty proceeds:
While bloody Sylla no mans blood will spare,
(The walles lament, and swellinge Tyber bleeds);
The Furies fury, fury slaughter breeds: 867
  Eight thousand Romans, Mithridates sped
  With one sad letter: and on bodies dead,
Through Vergell, did ye Punick wight his army lead.

105.

From Hell, Perillus fetcht his bull of brasse, 871
Wherin him-selfe first learnt to lowe and roare;

(The Italian Turk, and cannon, came thence.)

Th' Italian Turke from hence deriued was;
And army-murdringe peeces from this shore,
Were, by ye Spanish frier, brought in store: 875
  There Cain first learnt his brothers blood to spill;
  Herod, his endlesse fury to fullfill,
Had a decree from thence, ye tender babes to kill. 878

106.

[leaf 75]

Fond worldlinges then, that make a league with Hell,
As if thees quicke sands did not all beguile; 880
If so it were, ye Scythians sure did well
T' adore ye Fiend for feare, and those of Nile

To worshippe Ibis and ye Crocodile: 883
    But pride and tyrany together rise :
    Since Lucifer 's debarred from ye skies,
Hee in ye ayre his stratagems doth exercise. 886

107.

Witnesse distressed Maries sad estate, 887   *Mary is in sad estate.*
Who erst with worldely happinnesse was blest,
And liu'd in Pleasures affluence of late :
But gnawinge Conscience, deuoy'd of rest,   *Conscience has turned her*
Her shorte-liu'd pleasure quickely dispossest, 891   *pleasure to misery.*
    Her former iollity, tormenting thought,
    Terrour of conscience, melancholy wrought
That misery,[1] and misery to Mercy brought. 894

---

[1] 'Misery' from R. It is torn out of H.

Mary Magdalens death to sinne
or
Her life in righteousnesse.
[PART II.]

108. (II. 1)[1]

<small>The occasion of Maries dispossession.</small>

Soe night with sable weedes 'gan disapeare,   895
So melancholy vanishd quite away ;
So ioy her chearfull countenance did reare,
So did the orient day-springe bringe the day,
And all the trees were clad with bloominge May :   899
    The gladsome wren sate carolinge ye while,
    And faine the Titmouse would the day beguile,
But vnderneath, the meadowes at y^r musicke smile. 902

109. (II. 2)

Why did the flowers blaze in wanton pride,   903
And pearke y^r heades aboue the tender stalkes ?
Why was the Mary-gold distended wide ?
Why sange the birds amonge[2] their leauy walkes ?
Why skipp'd the lambs vpon their steepy balkes ?   907

<small>Christ, in his course,</small>

    Certes, the welbeloued went that waye,
    The heire of heauen, from whose glorious ray
The Sun deriues his light, and Phosphorus ye daye. 910

110. (II. 3)

<small>[leaf 76, back] sees Mary.</small>

And as that way he went (thrice happy houre !)   911
He spy'd a mayde come tumblinge downe apace,

---

[1] The numbering of the Stanzas begins again with 1 in the MS, but it is carried on from Part I in this print, for convenience of reference, as *M. M.* st. 108, &c.

[2] Corrected to 'amid'.

PART II. THE SPIRITS IN MARY APPEAL TO CHRIST. 43

From toppe of hills, y^t to the heauen towre :
A hollowe voice he heard, y^t would aghast
A wandringe straunger, and the Spirits cast   915 *The Spirits in her cast her at His feet.*
   Her beauteous frame before his whiter feet,
   And boweinge to ye ground, (as it was meete,)
His maiesty with feigned salutations greete.   918

111. (II. 4)

Then with their vncouth hollow soundinge voice, 919
(Such language Hell had taught them longe agoe,)
They roare and crye aloude with hydeous noyse,
"Wee knowe thy name; and whence thou art, we   *The Spirits in Mary ask Christ*
   knowe :   *not to turn them*
O doe not vse vs licke a cruell foe!   923   *out of her.*
   Thou art the Sonne of God, for euer blest!
   Thou cam'st to saue ; then saue vs with ye rest,
And dispossesse vs not from out this balefull brest! 926

112. (II. 5)

"Wee bee ye harbingers of heauens ire,   927
Wee Mercuries vnto Astræa bright,
Wee punish sinners in ye lake of fire,
Wee giue thee reuerence, and homage right,
And dutifully tremble at thy sight ;   931 *They tremble and obey Him, the*
   While man doth mocke at heauens ofspringe still,
   Wee yeeld obedience to thy sacred will :
Thou art a springe of good ; oh, worke not vs this ill!" *Source of Good.*

113. (II. 6)

Wonder it is, y^t this accursed crue   935 [leaf 77]
Should knowe ye Sauiour, whom but few could knowe ; *For so hee is described in the*
Sure, they obseru'd his white and ruddy hue,   *Canticles :*
That made him cheefest of 10 thousand showe,   *and the diue'ls knowe the*
His lockes as blacke as rauen, and ye snowe 939 *Scriptures. Luk: 9:*
   Of his faire Doue-like eyes. His cheekes beneath
   Bedight with flowers, like beds of Spices breath ;
His lily lippes, pure myrrhe vnto his spouse bequeath.

PART II. CHRIST BIDS THE SPIRITS LEAVE MARY.

114. (II. 7)

Cantic: 5: 13:

His hands, gould ringes beset with Chrysolite; 943
His mouth, with sweetnesse fraught, and odours newe;
His belly vnder, like ye Iu'ry white,
All interchast with veins of Sappheirs blewe:
His pleasant countenance like Hermons dewe, 947
   His leggs and feete, like marble pillers rare
   On goulden sockets, yet by farre more faire:
His vestures, with y^r Casia perfum'd ye aire. 950

115. (II. 8)

Christ's robe.

A robe hee wore, like to his essence, pure; 951
That vndiuided; vndeuided hee:
No wonder then (though 't seemes a wonder, sure)
That gloomy hell withouten eyes can see,
Iesus alone ye holy one to bee, 955
   And ye Messias, y^t should sin deface:
   Such was his countenance and louely grace,
That they bewrayd his country, and his heau'nly race.

116. (II. 9)

[leaf 77, back]
Zanch: lib: 3: cap: 9: et: lib: 9: cap: 9:

Though thought be free, nor can ye Stygian frie 959
Enter ye chambers of our better parte,
(For y^t belonges to heau'ns all-seeinge eye,
To search ye reines, and vnderstand ye hearte,
Nor will he this vnto his foes imparte) 963
   Whither they through ye Sences windowes pry'd,
   Or this by reuelation espy'd:
They knewe our Sauiours thought, and what would them
   betyde. 966

117. (II. 10)

But thus ye subtill serpents him bespake, 967
Hopinge, of Mercy, mercy to obtaine:
Yet simple elues, y^r marke they did mistake,
And hopinge prayd, and prayinge prayd in vaine:

For hee, poore Adam's sonnes will rather gaine ; 971
  "You knowe me, (said hee) but I knowe not you ;
  And yet I knowe yee for a cursed crewe :
Then leaue your habitation, and seeke a newe! 974

Christ bids the Spirits quit Mary.

118. (II. 11)

Like as ye thunder on mount Sinai hearde, 975
With flashinge lightninges and shrill trumpets sounde,
The future nations of Salem feard,
And made them flie, or fall flat on the ground,
Soe doth ye thunder of his voice confounde 979
  The powers of hell, who from his glorious sight,
  Swellinge with rancor, blasphemies and spight,
Vnto y^r dungeon againe they take y^r flight. 982

The dispossession of the euill spirits.

119. (II. 12)

Soone as they tooke y^r leaue, y^t causd her thrall, 983
Downe sunke ye Damsell in amazement deepe,
(After an earth-quake, soe the ground doth fall,)
And soundinge, yeelded to a sencelesse sleepe,
Ne could shee speake a worde, ne could shee weepe : 987
  But he y^t conquered all the powers beneath,
  The Hell of sin, and sin of Hell, and Death,
Soone brought againe ye maydens pantinge, faintinge
    breath. 990

[leaf 78]

Mary sinks down.

120. (II. 13)

With milke-white hand, hee by ye hand her tooke, 991
And stayd her faintinge head, and bad her cheare :
The burninge feuer then her heart forsooke,
Instead of which there came a suddaine feare :
So, when ye night begins to disappeare, 995
  The dawinge of ye day with glimmeringe light,
  That seemeth vncouth to ye weaker sight,
One newly layd a sleepe, and new awakd doth fright.

Christ lifts her by the hand,

46   PART II.   MARY IS BIDDEN TO REPENT.   SHE DOES SO.

121. (II. 14)

But feare soone vanishd, when ye heauenly swan,   999
and comforts her. With Musicke of his voice did comforte giue;
And then to sue for fauour shee began,
And humbly craue y^t shee with him might liue,
That did her soule from Hell and death repreiue.   1003
   As yet he granted not her suite: but said,
   "Thy trespasses are pardoned (O maide)!
[¹ first, 'them'] Repent¹ thee; and to sin heere after, bee affrayd!"

122. (II. 15)

[leaf 75, back]   Thus did ye winged Perseus of ye skie   1007
Mary is rescued.   Deliuer our distress'd Andromede,
That nowe with greefe prœpar'd herselfe to dye
By ye waue-tossinge monster of ye sea,
The sea of Acheron: nowe Panopee,   1011
   With all her nimphes, scuddes on ye marble plaine;
   The storme is ouerblowne, and once againe
Daye triumphes ouer night, and pleasure ouer paine.   1014

123. (II. 16)

The ship, that erst was toss'd with winde and tyde;
Hath nowe ye port of quietnesse attaind;
The pilgrime wandringe through ye deserts wide,
Hath nowe at length a ioyefull harbour gaind;
And shee, that erst was pitied and plaind,   1019
The returne of a   Nowe weepes for ioy, and ioyes in sorrow true;
good conscience.   And faire Syneide is return'd to viewe
Her chambers, and to build ye palaces a newe.   1022

124. (II. 17)

No sooner had she entred, but ye mayde   1023
Felt a warme motion within her brest,
And hard a tongue (though none shee sawe) y^t sayd:
Mary is told to "Goe to ye courts of Wisedome, gentle guest;
seek Repentance. There seeke Repentance, and with her, find rest: 1027

PART II. SHE GOES TO THE PALACE OF WISDOM.

Repentance hath a flood, doth euer flowe,
A flood of brinish[1] teares and bitter woe,
That, bee thou n'er soe blacke, will make thee white as
   snowe." 1030

125. (II. 18)

Mary, aggladded at this ioyfull newes, 1031   [leaf 79]
Seekes for ye palaces of Sapience ;   Mary is guided
A siluer doue, ye way vnto her shewes,   to the Palace of Wisdom.
And with his bill giues her intelligence,
Soe that shee needs no conduct of ye sence, 1035
  And yet shee can not bee without it well.
  Such pleasure, by ye way shee goes, doth dwell,
'T is hard to bee conceiud, but harder farre to tell.

126. (II. 19)

The forrests were like fragrant Lebanon : 1039   Cantic: 4: 11:
Pome-granates sweete, and saffron there contend ;
Spiknarde and Camphire with browne Cinnamon ;   Wisedome
Calamus, Myrrhe and Aloes befreind   described by her forrest.
Th' enamourd ayre, and all about they send 1043
  Perfumes, exhaled from y^r spicy beds.
  And heere and there a springe of milke dispreads,
And hony-dewe ye sweeter shrubs of spices weds. 1046

127. (II. 20)

The riuers shind with oyle, and on ye shore 1047   On the shore are
Faire Margarites and costly iewells laye ;   pearls and jewels.
The land emboweled great mines of Ore,
And all a-longe ye tinne-decayinge way,
The goodly Cedars seem'd to bidde her stay : 1051
  These did her captiuated eyes delight ;
  The flowry beds detaine her feete so white,
And middle-sizëd shrubs her tender hands invite. 1054

---

[1] MS. 'brimish,' as below too, p. 54, l. 1232.

128. (II. 21)

<small>[leaf 79, back]</small>
<small>By the situation of her tower.</small>

But then a rarer spectacle shee spies, 1055
The tower of Wisedome, y^t did seeme to threat,
With highe-aspiringe toppe ye cloudy skies :
The ground-worke on a massy rocke was set,
That neither windes could hurt, nor waters great. 1059
   Sharpe prickinge thornes and thistles were before ;
   On each side, desarts waste, and wilde beasts roare ;
Beyond, a furious sea doth wrastle with ye shore. 1062

129. (II. 22)

Why standes it on a hill ?—her glorie's highe ; 1063
Why on a rocke ?—shee constant doth perseuer ;
<small>Wisdom's Palace.</small> Why thornes before it ?—hard aduersity
And spiny labour goe before her euer ;
Why seas beyond it ?—head-longe folly neuer 1067
   Is farre from daunger ; why on eyther side
   Desarts and beasts ?—if either way you slide,
Into a thousand toylesome Labyrinths you glide. 1070

130. (II. 23)

What should I of this palace more relate, 1071
That in it-selfe all beauties doth enfould ?
All there was pretious, and of highest rate,
And though all glist'red not, yet all was gould,
Or moulde as pure, or farre the purer mould. 1075
<small>By humility her porter.</small>   Watchfull Humility still kept ye dore,
   And none had entrance to ye courte, before
They crau'd her helpinge hand, and did her ayde
   implore. 1078

131. (II. 24)

<small>[leaf 80]</small>
Humility, instructions harbinger, 1079
Sorrowes glad ofspringe, mother of our peace,
Charities nurse, Religions fosterer,
Path-way to heauen, troubled soules release ;

PART II. WISDOM AND HER PROPERTIES DESCRIBED.   49

Prides great abater, vërtues great encrease, 1083
  Others by risinge, raize y^r high desires;
  But when shee lowest falls, shee most aspires;
Shee dulls ye sharpest swordes, and quenches flaminge
    fiers. 1086

132. (II. 25)

Magdalene entred with this happy guide; 1087
And all amazed at ye rasters[1] bright,   [1 ? rafters]
Stone-still shee stood, till Wisedome shee espy'd,
With her owne worke of needle-worke bedight:
Then while shee wonders, giue mee leaue to write 1091   By her own
  Of her, with whome ye Sun may not compare: personage.
  Doue-like her eyes; her lockes of curled haire,   Wised: Sal: 7: 29:
A flocke of kids, y^t on mount Gilead feedinge are 1094   Cantic: 4:

133. (II. 26)

Her temples, peices of Pomegranates seeme; 1095   The person of Wisdom described.
Her feet, like newe-wash'd sheepe, ordred arright;
Her lippes, a thred of scarlet, you would deeme;
Her necke, like Dauids tower, where men of might
Hange vp y^r Targets, all in open sight; 1099
  Her brests like two yonge roes of œquall age,
  Amid ye lilies that haue pasturage:
Her talke is euer comely, sweet her carriage. 1102

134. (II. 27)

Doth any, honours diadem admire? 1103   [leaf 80, back]
With her, immortall honours euer dwell.
Doth any, great possessions desire?
Her riches, fadinge treasures farre excell.   Her riches excel all other treasures.
Is any thirsty? shee's a liuinge well; 1107
  Shee makes ye weake man stronge, ye foolish wise;
  Shee lends ye lame man feete, ye blinde man eyes;
Shee feedes ye hungry soule, and clothes ye naked
    thighes. 1110

135. (II. 28)

By her properties.

Wisedome 's yᵉ best of thinges, th' immortal treasure,
The double booke of Nature and of grace,
Honour deuoyd of shame, and painelesse pleasure,
Pilot of life, and life of eu'ry place,
Nobles reiecter, raiser of yᵉ base, 1115
Falsehoods discouery, light of humaine sence,

Wised: Sal: 7: v: 25: 26:

The great Allmighties subtill influence,
Mirrour of maiesty, heauens purest Quintessence. 1118

136. (II. 29)

Oh that I might for euer heere abide, 1119

[¹ yᵗ = that]

Within yᵉ palaces, that¹ age out-last,
And stay with Mary hard by Wisedomes side;
How nimbly would yᵉ goulden numbers hast,
When of her Nectar I should sippe a tast. 1123
Hence did yᵉ waters of Castalian plaine
First issue forth, though in a purer vaine:
And shee, yᵉ Pallas is, of great Iehouahs braine. 1126

137. (II. 30)

[leaf 81]

But nowé, behould, a goodly company 1127
Of Wisedomes children stand about her round:

By her 2 chambers.

Two roomes shee hath, this lowe, the other highe:
Heere sate Prince Salomon, and Dauid crownd,
With thousands of his Saints in pleasure drownd. 1131

In them are all

There stood yᵉ Monarche of this tripple Isle:
The Destinies for euer on him smile.
Others there were, but fewe, or none appear'd yᵉ while, 1134

138. (II. 31)

Beside all those that fauour her essayes, 1135
Whom in her palaces shee highly grac't,

1122, 1123. In H., 'hast,' 'tast' have a final *e* put on by a later hand.

PART II. REPENTANCE DESCRIBED.   51

And crownd with garlands of immortall bayes,   *whom*
That soe y^r names might neuer be defact,   *Wisdom makes immortal.*
Nor by ye tyrany of time eract,   1139
  That they ye Muses with y^r fauour rayse,
  And, by ye trumpet of ye Muses prayse,
Out-weare all-wearinge time, and liue immortall dayes.

139. (II. 32)

But whither doe my wandringe numbers straye? 1143
Returne (yee Muses) to the path againe!
And yet, with Wisedome, well they wander may,
Better then walke right on with folly vaine.
Heere all ye while stoode Magdalene, soe faine 1147
  To meete Repentance: Wisedome at ye last   *By her inmate repentance.*
  With hand in hand (shee knew ye Damselles hast)   *Wisdom leads Mary to Repentance.*
Conductes her thither, where ye weepinge grace was
  plac't.   1150

140. (II. 33)

Streightly immured in a closet small,   1151   *[leaf 81, back] Repentance described by her closet.*
Repentance sate, with eyes still fixt on ground;
A-downe her cheekes ye tricklinge teares fall;
Her slender hands, her tender brest ywound;   *By her actions.*
And, (woe is me!) shee cries with sighinge sound: 1155
  Her carelesse-hanginge haire shee teares, her head   *By her attire.*
  Was crownd with thornes, with dust besprinkeled;
Her loynes with sacke-cloth girt, her feete vncouered

141. (II. 34)

Angells stood round about her, as her gard,   1159   *By her attendants.*
(Though to ye outwarde eye, they were not seene)
And what on earth was sayd, in heaun was hard,
And all her teares were kept in bottels cleane;
(Teares, though a signe, yet ease of sorrowes keene:)
  Her head was stayd by ye Angelique crewe,
  Who all besprinkled her with holy dewe,
That shee might neuer faint, but aye her plaints re-
  newe.   1166

E 2

142. (II. 35)

By her riuer of teares.
[¹ MS. first 'Christall.']

A Crystall¹ riuer swifte before her fled,   1167
(Noe other lookinge-glasse shee had, poore soule,)
Instead of waues, the teares lift vp y^r head,
And to ye muddy shore of sin they rowle,
Beatinge against ye rocke of scandalls fowle :   1171
   The water of it was exceedinge tarte,
   Sore to ye eyes, but saluinge to ye heart :
Thees streames, abundant teares to all sicke soules
   imparte.   1174

143. (II. 36)

[leaf 82]

Tears are Heaven's showers.

Teares, ye Soules bath, ye weepinge oliue tree ;   1175
Teares, cause of comforte, though effect of greefe ;
Teares, heauens showers, ye dewe of Iris bee,
Teares, amonge Paradises riuers cheefe,
Teares, Pœnitences badge, and hearts releife ;   1179
   Teares bee ye sinner's solitary sporte ;
   Teares, hopefull sorrowe's longe-desired port ;
Teares, handmaides to Repentance in Astræas courte.

144. (II. 37)

Repentance is the way to Life.

Repentance is ye way to life by death ;   1183
Repentance, health giu'n in a bitter pill ;
Repentance, hearbe of grace, diuiner breath ;
Repentance, rectifier of the will ;
Repentance, loue of good, and hate of ill ;   1187
   Repentance, mirth at last, though first annoy ;
   Repentance, Ibis, y^t doth snakes destroye ;
Repentance, earth's debate, heau'ns darlinge Angels
   ioye.   1190

145. (II. 38)

Teares quench ye thunder-bolts of zeale diuine,   1191
Repentance makes ye cruellst foe repent :

Tears purify,

Teares keepe from putrefaction with y^r brine,
Repentance sharpe, but sweetend by content :

Teares earthly, yet vnto ye heauen[1] sent; 1195   and lead to heaven.
  Repentance euer doth ye worke begin :   [1 MS. first 'heauns']
  Teares follow her, and cleanse ye sinke of sin :
Come, come, ye Saints, a pace! and with Repentance
  inne. 1198

146. (II. 39)

Desire's ye cause of Sin ; Sin, cause of greefe ; 1199   [leaf 82, back]
Greife bids repent, Repentance bringes forth teares ;   The cause of Marie Magdalenes repentance.
Teares, pitie mooue, and pitty graunts releife,
That comforte, comforte hope, which nothinge feares ;
Hope leades to faith, faith to ye Sauiour reares : 1203
  Iesus, to blisse, his militants doth raize ;
  Blisse causes glory, glory ends in prayse ;
Prayse ends in him, y^t no begininge knew, nor end of
  dayes. 1206

147. (II. 40)

This made ye Damsell in distressed state, 1207
Hopinge in teares to drench her misery,
Stand waitinge still at Pœnitence's gate :
Where, when shee knockt, Repentance by and by
Demaunded, whoe was there ; shee made replie : 1211
  A sinfull soule.—(*Rep.*) Then must you not come   The true repentance is a turninge from sin.
    heere.
  (*Magdal.*) Oh, let me in (sweet Grace !) you need not
    feare.
(*Rep.*) Thou wilt defile my bridall chamber.—(*Mag.*)
  I am cleare. 1214

148. (II. 41)

(*Rep.*) Cleare ? Whoe hath cleard thee, or with gracious
  light 1215
Illumined thy minde?—(*Magd.*) The holy one.
(*Rep.*) Where bee ye Spirits of Infernall night,
That whilome thee possest?—(*Mag.*) Oh ; they are
  gone.

PART II. MARY PLEADS WITH REPENTANCE.

(*Repent.*) Where bee thy louers?—(*Mag.*) I am heere alone. 1219
(*Rep.*) If I admit thee, wilt thou not repent?

Mary promises to be firm in her repentance.

(*Magd.*) Repent I neuer will.—(*Rep.*) To what intent Should I then let thee in, if thou wilt n'er repent?

149. (II. 42)

[leaf 83]

(*Magd.*) Oh yes, I will repent me of my sin; 1223
But of Repentance I will n'er repent.
(*Rep.*) What wilt thou doe, if y^t I let thee in?
(*Mag.*) With sorrowes due, I'll paye thee yearly rent.
(*Rep.*) What diœt wilt thou haue?—(*Mag.*) Sighes to relent. 1227
(*Rep.*) They're too stronge-breath'd.—(*Ma.*) Fitter for my weake plaint.—
(*Rep.*) What more?—(*M.*) Fewe teares. (*Rep.*) y^r heat will make thee faint.
(*M.*) I freeze. (*Rep.*) They coulder are. (*M.*) I burne.
(*Rep.*) Come in, poore Saint! 1230

150. (II. 43)

Mary Magdalens repentance.
[¹ MS. brimish]
In teares.

Soe in shee came, directed by her guide, 1231
And dipt her finger in ye brinish¹ well,
And with her eyes ye sharpnesse of it try'd,
From whence ye teares, as thicke as showers, fell,
And raisd ye bubles of ye watry cell, 1235
 As when a doubtfull cloud dissolus his raine,
 Into ye ample bosome of ye maine:
His showers, her teares, y^t fell, seeme all to fall in vaine. 1238

151. (II. 44)

In gesture.

Her head hunge downe, (heauy it was with greefe,)
Nor durst shee euer looke vp to ye skie: 1240
Of sinners shee esteem'd herselfe ye cheefe,
And knewe ye wrath of heauens maiesty.

PART II. MARY LAMENTS HER FORMER SINS.   55

Fast on ye moystened floore, shee cast her eye,   1243
  And eu'ry where shee findes some cause to plaine,
But still Syneide comforts her againe,   *Conscience com-*
And tells her, y^t ye lambe, for sinners must bee slaine.   *forts Mary.*

152. (II. 45)

At length a rufull voice her silence brake,   1247   [leaf 88, back]
Like swellinge waters, troubled with ye winde,
And thus with greefe of heart ye Damsell spake,   *In sorrowefull*
" Ah, foolish woman, to thy selfe vnkinde !   *eiaculations.*
When others see, howe longe hast thou been blinde? 1251
  Witnesse ye flash of pleasure for a while,
  That, with ye falshehood of a guilded smile,
Did thee, poore wretch, allure ; alluringe, did beguile.

153. (II. 46)

" Vaine pleasure, cause of endlesse paine, adieu ! 1255   *Conscience shows*
Sweete is thy baite, but deadly is thy baine,   *Mary the vanity*
When for an howres delight, an age wee rue,   *of Pleasure.*
An ounce of mirth procures a world of paine,
And pleasure in his infancy is slaine :   1259
  The swellinge bubble, sweet flower, springinge grasse,
  Falls, fadeth, is not, what but now it was :
But shorter pleasure, all in shortnesse doth surpasse."

154. (II. 47)

Thus shee laments, and while shee casts her eyes   1263
Vpon ye water, y^t was vnder plac'd,
Her gentle shadowe, mourninge shee espies,   *In occasioninge*
And all ye beauty of her face defac'd :   1266   *of lamentation.*
" Oh, hadst thou euer, (sayes shee) thus been grac'd,
  Beauty, thou rocke of Soules, faire Sirens smile,
  Nights glitteringe glowe-worme, wepinge Crocodile.
Beauty more lou'd then purest gould, then drosse more
     vile.   1270
      1268. Rawl. reads " Hellen's."

56   PART II. MARY LAMENTS HER FORMER SINS.

155. (II. 48)

[leaf 84]

"And yet ye pourtract of this outward frame,   1271
The rarest gifte, y^t euer from aboue
Heau'n did on earth bestowe, had not y^t shame
Of wretched man with-drawne his makers loue:
For, saue his soule infused by ye Doue,   1275
  What else in man worth note?—vnhappy fall.
Since when (but whoe can date expir'd recall?)
That which is best in vs, wee make it worst of all. 1278

156. (II. 49)

In acknowledg-
inge her former
misdemeanor.

"Thees haires, y^t modestly should haue beene ty'd 1279
(For modesty 's a maydes best ornament)
Layd out in tresses, haue declar'd my pride:
Thees eyes were made to viewe ye firmament,
And giue Him glory, y^t such glory lent.   1283

Mary's eyes have
been wanton.

But (woe is mee!) they haue ye glasses beene,
  Where folly lookd, and wantonnesse was seene,
Soe ioyfull to attend vpon ye Cyprian Queene.   1286

157. (II. 50)

"Thees cheekes should blush at sin with crimson die,
But they to lewdnesse cheefely doe inuite,

Her smiles have
tempted the
onlooker.

With smiles deceiuinge ye beheulders eye:
Thees lippes were made to prayse, and pray arright,
Not to delude ye soone-deluded sight: 1291
  This tongue should singe out Halleluiahs,
  Not accent vaine lasciuious essayes:
Hands, feet, heart, all were made, to speake y^r makers
    prayse.   1294

158. (II. 51)

"But I (poore wretch! such wretches, sinners bee), 1295
Led captiue by ye powers of Hell beneath,
Each member haue defild, noe parcell free,
And liuinge, entred in ye snares of death,

PART II. MARY CONFESSES HER OLD EVIL WAYS. 57

Vnworthy then to drawe this vitall breath. 1299
 Oh that I might those yeares againe recall, *She wishes she*
 That made me free to Sin in Pleasures thrall." *could recall her ill-spent days.*
Yet better late repente, then not repent at all : 1302

159. (II. 52)

No siluer haires her goulden twist had chang'd, 1303 [leaf 84, back]
No pallid hue assaild her rosy-red,
No wrinkles had her browe from loue estraung'd,
No rottenesse her Iu'ry teeth be-spread :
Youth in his freshest colours flourished. 1307
 And yet shee thought, in humblenesse of minde, *In humblenesse.*
 The dayes to longe, y^t had her thus confin'd,
Repentance, with ye least offence, some falt can finde.

160. (II. 53)

Thus in her selfe, her selfe shee wellnigh lost, 1311
And on her selfe her sighes and sorrowes spent ;
Till ye next roome her cogitations crost,
With pearly teares and Crystall[1] due besprent, *Mary weeps,*
And gaue her store of matter to lament : 1315 *and shows her repentance.*
 Then shee begins a-fresh, (for to her thought [1 MS. first 'Christall']
 Thees spectacles ye courts of Pleasure brought,
Where ill was counted good, and good was counted
 naught.) 1318

161. (II. 54)

" Faire courtes without, but foulest sinkes within, 1319 *In detestinge of*
Vnder your roofes, would I had neuer beene ! *her sinfull life.*
Sweet sportes, but leauend with a lumpe of Sin !
Would God, I neuer had your madnesse seene !
And thou, vaine Pleasure, youths adored queene, 1323
 Oh, maist thou euer bound in hell remaine,
 And suffer torments of œternall paine !
For thou hast ship-wrackt all, and many a Soule hast
 slaine. 1326

58 PART II. MARY PREFERS THE HARDSHIPS OF PENITENCE.

162. (II. 55)

[leaf 85]
She would rather be shut up, than left free to sin.

"Better it is with-in this narrowe roome   1327
To spend our flittinge dayes, and closely keepe,
Then, while wee liue, soe fairely to intombe
Our soules in Marble pleasures, y^t will weepe
Dayes without end, when wee haue tooke our sleepe.
  Better, this well of teares, then clearest founts,
  For sad Repentance, in true ioye surmounts
  Vaine Pleasures shady bowers, sweet gardens, rich
    accounts.   1334

163. (II. 56)

"Better thy thorne-bush then a crowne of Myrtle, 1335
Thy ashes, better then ye bread of strife;
Better thy sacke-cloth, then a silken kirtle;
Thy bitter, better then ye sweetest life;
Better thy selfe, then is ye rarest wife :   1339

Repentance is the key of Heaven.

  Repentance, hearts content, ye sinners stay,
  The salt of all our actions, ye key
That opens heau'n, and leads into ye courts of day. 1342

164. (II. 57)

"The hate of sinfull life, and sorrowes deepe,   1343
Surpasse ye loue of life, and life of loue :
For what is y^t which wantons 'loue' yclepe,
But hot desires y^t doe each passion mooue,
And through ye veines with lust-full poyson roaue;
  A foolish fancy and a pleasinge paine,
  That dimmes ye eyes, and dulls ye purest braine. 1349
But loue, from heauen came, and thither goes againe."

165. (II. 58)

[leaf 85, back]
Mary stops weeping,

So nowe, me thinkes, her waylinge should be done, 1351
The closets shutt, ye liquid fountaine drie;
Herselfe, loue, pleasure, shee hath ouer-run,
Yet downe her cheekes ye Isicles doe hie,

PART II. NATURE REMINDS MARY OF HER SINS. 59

Though sad laments and waylinge accents die: 1355
  Sighes serue for voice, teares for a tongue, to showe
  The meaninge of her minde, and inward woe: *and goes out with Repentance.*
And when all's done, abroad shee and Repentance goe.

166. (II. 59)

And as they walke abroad in open aire, 1359
Each thinge shee spies, is matter of her teares:
The creatures with her-selfe shee doth compare;   *In contemplation.*
And when ye Sun in bright array appeares,
He blushes at her shame; and when shee heares 1363
  The chirpinge birds, she thinkes they doe reioyce
  To see her weepe, and heare her broken voice;
And vpon her alone, ye beasts to gaze make choyse.

167. (II. 60)

As by she passes, each tree shakes his head, 1367 *All Nature seems to reproach Mary.*
Notinge her shame, and infamy of life:
The flowers turne, and seeme refuse her tread;
The buzzinge flies about are very rife;
The winde, against her, blowes with mickle strife:
  But to herselfe most sharpe, she rents her haire,
  Showringe forth teares, with sighes and humble prayer, *Ioyn'd with sighes and prayer.*
So to content ye earth with teares, with sighes ye aire.

168. (II. 61)

Then a newe contemplation shee invents, 1375 *[leaf 86]*
(But all her contemplations holy were,)
And thus with piteous mone shee sore laments,
Holdinge her hands vp to ye spangled sphære:
"Oh thou y^t guidst thy burninge horses there, 1379
  Thy state I envie, sith thy race is run
  From East to West, and mine scarse yet begun;
My darknesse, others blindes; to others, shines y^e
  Sun.

60 PART II. MARY CONTRASTS NATURE WITH HER OLD EVIL LIFE.

169. (II. 62)

She contrasts its sweet scents

"Sweete is yᵉ smell, yᵗ fragrant flowers bringe, 1383
Wouinge yᵉ winde to kisse them once againe;
Sweet are yᵉ notes, yᵗ birds sit carolinge
To him yᵗ made them; but yᵉ filthy staine

with her foul sin.

Of sin hath mee disodour'd, and my straine 1387
Tunes nought but vanity and fond delight:
The grasse with freshest colours is bedight;
The trees bringe fruit: but fruitlesse I, as darke as
  night. 1390

170. (II. 63)

"The fire hath heat, but I was dead in sin: 1391
The aire is moist, my vertue withered:
Solid yᵉ earth: but I haue euer been
Vnstable: water coole; I, tortured

[leaf 86, back]

With burninge lust: All haue perseuered 1395

Nature has obeyed God. Mary has wrought only ill.

In true obedience, performinge still,
What was inioyn'd them first by heauens will,
While I, vnhappy soule, haue wrought no worke but [ill.]

171. (II. 64)

In her wishes.

"Oh that mine eyes a fountaine weare of teares, 1399
That I might cleanse my sin-polluted soule,
Or yᵗ my dayes were like yᵉ Eagles yeares,
That with my age I might renewe my smarte,
So should Repentance neuer from mee parte!" 1403
But oh, enough (faire Damsell), though yᵉ skies
Nor yᵉ vast sea with water can suffice
To purge our sin, yet faith from heauen biddes thee rise."

172. (II. 65)

Mary hears that Jesus is at the Pharisee's house.

So shee arrose, and by yᵉ way heard tell, 1407
That Iesus with yᵉ Pharise nowe sate:
Thrice happy messenger, yᵗ came so well,
Such vnexpected tidinges to relate,

PART II. SHALL MARY GO TO JESUS AT THE PHARISEE'S? 61

And helpe a sinner in distress'd estate! 1411
    Yet shee was daunted at y̆ᵉ Pharise,
  (For Pharises and sinners n'er agree,
Though Pharises themselues, of s[i]nners cheefest bee).

173. (II. 66)

A while shee pauzinge stood, and 'gan to doubt, 1415 [leaf 87]
Whither shee to y̆ᵉ Pharises should goe,
Or rather for her Sauiour staye without;
(Such men bee of austere regarde, wee knowe,
And to y̆ᵉ vulgar make a goodly showe.) 1419
  But other thoughts, to quell this care begin,
  "The Pharise's a man, and men haue sin;
Then, bee hee n'er so good, a better is within. 1422

She doubts whether she should go there.

174. (II. 67)

"A better is within, and hee so good, 1423
That howe maye I, polluted soule, come neare?
Women defiled with a fluxe of blood,
Maye not amonge y̆ᵉ hallowed appeare:
I am vnclean, and leprous eu'ry where, 1427 *She is unclean.*
  How shall I then approach before his eye,
  More bright then is [y̆ᵉ] Eagle's, y̆ᵗ doth prie
Into y̆ᵉ cabinets of deepest secrecy?— 1430

175. (II. 68)

"But yet in mercy is his cheefe delight: 1431 [leaf 87, back]
Hee came to heale y̆ᵉ sicke, to saue y̆ᵉ lost;
Hee cur'd 10 Lepres, gaue y̆ᵉ blinde y̆ʳ sight,
Feet to y̆ᵉ lame, life to y̆ᵉ nummed ghost,
Speech to y̆ᵉ dumbe, and comforte to y̆ᵉ moste: 1435
  And, which with prayse must euer bee confest,
  (Blest be y̆ᵉ time! his name for euer blest!)
Seu'n sprights, with thunder hee ycharm'd from out my
    brest. 1438

Mary recounts the good deeds of Jesus.

176. (II. 69)

    "Certes his loue will couer all my shame,   1439
And with his robe my errours I may hide:
For I am sicke, lost, leprous, blinde, and lame,
Dumbe, comforteles, and dead: nor is it pride,
To seeke for helpe: then, what so'er betide,   1443
    Thither I'l goe! if Christ once bidde me stay,
    The Pharise can neuer say mee nay:
Oh, happy place, where heau'n hath placd another day!"

She resolves to go to Him at the Pharisee's.

177. (II. 70)

A boxe of costely odours shee præpar'd,   1447
Odours t' anoynt[1] th' anoynted from aboue,
And with it streight to Simons house shee far'd,
With true repentance to declare her loue:
Shee brake it, and ye roome could soone approoue 1451
    The fragrant smell: such is a contrite heart,
    That to ye heau'n sweet sauours doth impart,
The oyntment of good workes, and pænitence, ne'r parte.

[leaf 88]
[1 H. anotnt]
In her charity.

178. (II. 71)

Præpared thus, behinde his feet shee stood,   1455
Dissolu'd in teares of sweet (though bitter) brine,
And with ye torrent of a Chrystall[1] flood,
Shee wash'd his feet, his iu'ry feet diuine,
And then shee wip'd them with ye goulden twine 1459
    Of her dissheuel'd haires: full many a kisse
    Shee gaue, and tooke; and, conscious of y^r blisse,
Her lippes waxt pale, for feare they had done ought amisse.   1462

Luk: 7: 38:
In her behauiour.
[1 MS. first 'Christall']
Mary washes Christ's feet: wipes them with her hair, and kisses them.

179. (II. 72)

That falt, ye willinge maide will soon amend,   1463
For lauishely shee powres her oyntement sweet,
(Though lauishely enough shee n'er could spend
That which shee spent vpon his heau'nly feet:)

[leaf 88, back]
Then she anoints them.

PART II. MARY AT SIMON'S HOUSE, KISSING JESUS' FEET.   63

So did her misery his mercy greet:　　　　　　1467
　Sweet was thy vnction (Mary), sweet thy kisse,
　But sweetest of all sweetes, thy teares (I-wis):
The onely waye to heauen, by salt water is.　　1470

180. (II. 73)

Happy wert thou to touch ye tressells bare　　1471　*Happy she to touch and kiss her Saviour's body so!*
Of thy beloued, heau'nly paramour,
With eye, with hand, with temples, lippe and haire:
Yet thrice more happy, sith thy Sauiour,
With eye, heart, hand of faith thou didst adore:　1475
　So doth a loue-sicke soule of best desarte,
　Desire to touch her louer in each part,
And closely steale his body, y^t hath stole her heart.

181. (II. 74)

Oyntement shee mingles aye with bitter teares;　1479　[leaf 89]
Teares with sweet oyntement aye shee doth confound:　*She sheds bitter tears.*
No better balme in Gilead appeares,
No sweeter smell in Lebanons rich ground:
This saints ye sinner, makes ye sickest sound:　1483
　Oyntement and teares (if true) to get her inne,
　First ope ye sluce, and shed teares for thy sin,
Then to anoynt Christe's feet, with Magdalen begin. 1486

182. (II. 75)

Humility, lowe at his feet biddes stand;　　　1487　*Reflections on Mary's acts.*
Behinde him, rosy-blushinge Modesty:
Teares for his feet, Repentance doth commaund;
And Selfe-Hate, with her haire biddes make them drie:
Loue biddes her kisse, and Liberality　　　　1491
　Wills her to breake ye boxe, and oyntement powre.
　Hardenes of heart, pride, shamelesnesse before,
Lust, luxury, selfe-loue, possess'd her thoughts of yore.

PART II. 'AN APOSTROPHE TO CHRISTE.'

183. (II. 76)

[leaf 89, back]

Mary at Jesus' feet.

Mee thinkes, I see yᵉ Damsell at her worke, 1495
While shee embalmes his feet with odours rare;
With modest blush, howe shee hath learnt to lurke,
And kisse his feet, his marble feet, so faire,
And then to wipe them with her carelesse haire : 1499
   Often her hands, often her lippes, came near[e];
   Oft wipes shee of yᵉ oyntement, yᵗ I feare,
The oyntement wanted sweet, his feet perfumed weare.

184. (II. 77)

Her ointment and the Nectar of His feet are more precious than Simon's good cheer.

Yet sweet yᵉ oyntement was, though sweeter farre 1503
The Nectar of his feet, with dewe besprent :
So weake perfumes (though sweet) soone drowned are,
If they bee mingled with a deper sent :
Simons good cheare giues no such good content : 1507
   His ghuests are frolicke with yʳ dainty meat;
   But shee delights yᵉ brinish teares to eat,
And ioyeth more in hers, then they in highest seat. 1510

185. (II. 78)

[leaf 90]

An apostrophe to Christe.

[yʳ = their]

Some at feast haue crau'd thy company; 1511
But fewe or none, sweet oyntement for thee kept;
Some haue anoynted, but fewe wip'd the[e] drie :
Some wip'd thee drie; but wipinge, fewe haue wept;
Beyond them all, kinde Magdalene hath stept : 1515
   Some on thy head bestow'd yʳ charity,
   (Such was yᵉ vse in auncient times,) but shee,
Oyntinge thy feet, from toppe to toe anoynted thee. 1518

186. (II. 79

Would that I could do as St. Thomas or Mary did!

O, that I might, with waueringe Thomas, dippe 1519
The finger of my faith within his side,
Or heere with Magdalene obtaine a sippe,
(Farre from my humble thought bee greater pride !)

PART II. JESUS CLEANSES MARYS SIN, AND CHEERS HER. 65

From out his feet, with pleasures beautified ; 1523
  What would hee giue for weepinge Maries place,   *Lips: in theatr:*
  Whose hermitinge humility could grace   *honor: Iesuit:*
The Linnen cloutes, y^t did our Sauiours wound embrace.

187. (II. 80)

Faine would I leaue of Maries loue to writ[e], 1527 *I must write still*
But still her loue y^t will not let me leaue :   *of Mary's love.*
In loue shee liu'd, and now with loues delight,
Her former loue, y^t did her eyes deceiue,
In-stead of loue, of life shee doth bereaue : 1531
  Faire mayde, redeemed from ye iawes of Hell,
  Howe hardly can I bidde thy loue fare-well !
That which thou lou'st to doe, so doe I loue to tell. 1534

188. (II. 81)

The Pharisæ y^t thought hee sawe, was blinde ; 1535 *[leaf 90, back]*
The abiect sinner had the clearer eye ;
For thus hee reasoned within his minde ;
' Were this a Prophet, hee would soone descrie   *Simon doubts*
The wickednesse of her y^t standes so nighe :' 1539 *Jesus being a Prophet.*
  Thus hee coniectur'd, yet hee vtter'd nought :
  But his hypocrisie to light was brought ;
For well hee knewe her former life, y^t knewe his
    thought. 1542

189. (II. 82)

Then hee begins her action to commend 1543
To Simon in a parable of debt,
And sayes vnto him : " Seest thou her, my freind ?   *Jesus shows*
Great is her loue, because her Sin is great :   *Simon how Mary's love exceeds his.*
To washe my feet, no water hast thou set ; 1547
  But shee with teares hath washt them : on my head
  Thou hast not powred oyle : but shee, in-stead,
With costly oyntement hath my feet be-sprinkeled. 1550
MARY MAGDALENE.
     F

190. (II. 83)

Jesus pardons and blesses Mary.

"No kisse thou gau'st mee for a kinde salute; 1551
But shee vnto my feet doth kisses giue:
So her affection with her smiles doe sute:
Thy sinns (sayth hee) are cleansd, and thou shalt liue:
Goe hence in peace, sweete mayde! for euer thriue!"
 Wonder it is, y^t hee, whose sacred might 1556
 May call all prayse and glory, his by right,
Should giue such heaunly prayse vnto a mortall wight.

191. (II. 84)

[leaf 91]

In her religious duties.

Away shee went, aggladded at the heart, 1559
(Packe hence all sorrowe, let ye Damsell cheare!)
Yet so, y^t neuer from him shee would parte:
And nowe her browe and cheekes began to cleare,
And ioye displayd his banners eu'ry where; 1563
 Now with a shole of Maries so deuout,
 Shee ministers, and deales her goods about,
And followes her Leige-Lorde ye villages throughout.

192. (II. 85)

Mary listens to all Christ says.

Nowe on his rarest miracles shee gazeth, 1567
And with attention shee likes to heare,
While hee ye lustre of his light eblazeth,
And charmes with sacred eloquence each eare.
So shee awaited still, both farre and neare, 1571
 Till death approach'd, and hee inuaded Hell:
 But of his death, what should I further tell?
Better maye hee that sange his birth, ringe out his knell.

193. (II. 86)

Mary anoints Christ's corpse.

Many a teare in Golgotha shee spent, 1575
To waile his torment and her owne distresse;
And after, hied her to his monument,
With odours sweet his wounded corps to dresse:

1566. *throughout:* Rawl. about.

PART II. MARY MAGDALENE AT CHRIST'S TOMB. 67

In life shee lou'd him, and in death no lesse.   1579
　The earth was clad with sable weeds of night
　When Magdalene, so full of rufull plight,
Prœuents ye daye, and in ye darke seekes for her light.   Joh: 20: 1:

194. (II. 87)

O blessed woman, without Paragon,   1583   [leaf 91, back]
That couldst outrun (such is ye force of loue)
The faithefull Peter and beloued Iohn,
And bee ye first y^t sawe ye stones remoue!
This boone was graunted thee from heau'n aboue: 1587   Her loue to Christe, and sorrowe for his death.
　But when shee could not finde his body there,
　Shee runs to them, and cries with piteous feare,
"Aye mee! my lord is gon! and layd, wee knowe not
　where."   1590

195. (II. 88)

Iohn faster ran, but Peter farther went: 1591
Hee came vnto ye sepulchre, and stayd;
The other entred in ye monument;
But both out-stripped by ye weepinge mayde:
They sawe ye linnen clothes and kercheife layd   1595
　A-part: but shee, ye Angells first did viewe,   Mary sees the Angels first.
　As downe shee bow'd, in weeds of whitest hue.
Poore Mary knewe not them, although they Mary
　knewe.   1598

196. (II. 89)

Shee drownes her-selfe in teares of saltest brine;   1599
They aske her, why shee weepes, and makes such mone:
Shee sayes, "my Lorde is taken from this shrine;"
And hauing sayd, shee spies her Lord alone;
And yet to her, though seen, hee is not knowne: 1603
"Woman! (sayes hee) why makst thou such laments?"
　Shee aunswerd, "Sir! if thou hast borne him hence,   Mary asks Christ where her Lord is laid.
　Tell mee but where hee lies, and I will fetch him thence."

　　1580. H. and R. read "might," which I suppose is a mistake of the copyist.

F 2

MARY SEES CHRIST RISEN. ALL REJOICE.

197. (II. 90)

[leaf 92]
Mary thinks Christ is the Gardener.

Shee thought her Lorde, ye gardiner had been: 1607
And keeper of a garden, sure, was hee:
Yet no such garden, where dead sculls are seen,
But Paradise, where pleasures euer bee,
And blisse deriu'd from lifes aye-liuinge tree: 1611
   Thither ye theife and he together went,
   And thither Mary must at length bee sent;
But first ye dimme light of her life must needs bee spent.

198. (II. 91)

Shee, to anoynt his breathlesse body came; 1615
With oyle of gladnesse hee, to oynt her head:
To keepe him from corruption, was her ayme;
His purpose was to raise her from ye dead.

Christ calls her by her name.

By name hee call'd her (happily shee sped!) 1619
   To bee the messenger of heau'[n]ly newes,
   That gladdes the heart, and fadinge age renewes,
And to ye Saints, thinges longe time vnreueiled shewes.

199. (II. 92)

She tells the Saints that He has risen.

Awaye shee postes, all rauish'd with desire, 1623
And to ye Saints together met, shee hies:
Her tidings make y^e trobled soules admire;
And yet her solace, and sweet obloquies,
Make constant hope, and better thoughts arrise. 1627
   Their prayses loud vp to y^e heau'ns they send:

All rejoice.

   Ioye closes all, (such ioye no style hath penn'd)
So end I with y^r ioye; ner may y^t ioye haue end! 1630

$\Delta o\xi a \; \tau \widehat{\omega} \; \vartheta \epsilon \widehat{\omega}.$

DE CHRISTO CUM SIMONE PHARISÆO PRANDENTE, ET MARIAM MAGDALENAM COMITER EXCIPIENTE.

Quid petit angustas epulas Simonis Iesus,
   Qui sua Nectareis proluit ora cadis?
Non opus est illi mortalibus: ille tuetur,
   Quicquid habet tellus, æquora quicquid habent:
Forsitan haud cupiit ditis conviuia mensæ,
   Sed cupiit lacrymas præscius (alma) tuas:
Credo, insulsa forent tua nam conviuia Simon,
   Magdala in tepidum funderet vsque salem.

FLET: RIDET

AD MARIAM MAGDALENAM.

Cum video risum porrecta fronte serenum,
   Cum video lacrymas (alma puella) tuas,
Sic reputo: certè omen habet, seu riserit amens
   Magdala, sine etiam Magdala fleuit amans:
Sunt avi violenta breuis: nam gaudia luctum
   Tanta ferunt, tantus gaudia luctus habet:
Vt fleat alternum, mihi sic risisse videtur,
   Sic flere, vt tandem rideat illa magis.

AD EANDEM.

Magdala, quid miserè lacrymarum flumina fundis?
   Perfundis liquido quid tibi rore genas?
Abluis anne pedes Domini? sed sorde carebant;
   Abluis an culpam (non caret illa) tuam?
An sic Angelicos vtres implere requiris?
   An sic cœlestes pura videbis aquas?
O sale macte tuo: tibi Spiritus, aura fecunda est,
   Anchora, spes audax, carbasa, laeta fides.

T. R.

Laus Deo.

NOTES.

α. NOTES TO THE DEDICATORY LINES WHICH ARE ONLY IN THE HARLEIAN MANUSCRIPT.

40. *Persius*, Flaccus Aulus, a Latin poet of Volaterræ, was of an equestrian family, and made himself known by his intimacy with the most illustrious Romans of the age. He distinguished himself by satirical humour, and made the faults of the orators and poets of his time the subject of his poems. He died A.D. 62.

52. *Harrington*, James, an eminent political writer, was born in 1611, being the eldest son of Sir Lapcote Harrington. When he made progress in classical learning, he was admitted, in 1629, a gentleman-commoner of Trinity College, Oxford, etc. He made some attempts in the poetical way. In 1658 he published an English translation of two eclogues of Virgil, and two books of the *Æneis*, and in 1659 was printed his translation of the four following books of the *Æneis*; but his poetry gained him no reputation as his political writings did. See *Biographica Britannica; Athen. Oxon.* vol. ii., and Chalmers's *Biograph. Dictionary*.

64. *Aratus*, a Greek poet of Cilicia; about 277 B.C. He was greatly esteemed by Antigonus Gonatus, king of Macedonia, at whose court he passed much of his time, and at whose request he wrote a poem on astronomy, comprehended in 1154 verses, in which he gives an account of the situations, rising, setting, number, and motion of the stars. Cicero represents him as unacquainted with astrology, yet capable of writing upon it in elegant and highly-finished verses, which, however, from the subject, admit of little variety. Aratus wrote also hymns and epigrams, etc.

St. Paul, when addressing the philosophers of Athens in the Areopagus, quotes the exordium of Aratus's *Phenomena* (Acts xvii. 28. For *in him we live, and move, and have our being:* as certain also of *your own poets have said,* For we are also his offspring). "Although the sacred historian only gives four words as a reference to the passage, it is likely that St. Paul quoted some more, to prove to his learned audience that the doctrine of the eternity, unity, and omnipotence of the Godhead was no new invention, or confined to the Jewish nation, but the creed of the wisest of their own philosophers and poets."

English translations of his works are: *a.* Jabez Hughes, Translations from Aratus in his *Miscellanies in Prose and Verse*. Lond. 1737. β *The Phenomena and Diosemeia*, translated into English verse, with notes, by J. Lamb. Lond. 1848. γ. *The Skies and Weather Forecasts of Aratus*, translated, with notes, by E. Poste. Lond. 1880.

66. *Lucan*, Roman poet of the Augustan age, died A.D. 65.

88. *Chrysostom*[e], a bishop of Constantinople, who died A.D. 407, in his 53rd year. He was a great disciplinarian, and by severely lashing the vices of his age, he procured himself many enemies. He was banished for opposing the raising a statue to the Empress Eudoxia, the wife of Arcadius, after having displayed his abilities as an elegant preacher, a sound theologian, and a faithful interpreter of Scripture. His works appeared in 1718 in 13 vols. fol., Paris, ed. Benedict. Mountfaucon.

89. *Prudentius*, Aurelius Clemens, a Latin poet, who flourished A.D. 392, and was successively a soldier, an advocate, and a judge. His poems are numerous, and all theological, devoid of the elegance and purity of the Augustan age, and yet greatly valued for the zeal which he manifests in the cause of Christianity, and for the learning and good sense which he everywhere displays. He lived a great age, and his piety was rewarded by the highest offices in the Church. His works appeared at Paris, 1687, ed. The Delphin.

β. NOTES TO "THE LIFE AND DEATH OF MARY MAGDALENE."

4. *debellish* = embellish (Fletcher).

7. *spiny* = thorny.

12. *needs* is here the old adverb *necessarily*

41. *greeces:* obs. term for steps.

54. *Alcides:* a name of Heracles, either from his strength (ἀλκή) or from his grandfather *Alcœus*.

64. *in lue of*, in lewe of = au lieu de.

69. *Falern:* on the south-west coast of Italy, famous for its wine.

70. *Thyme of Hybla:* Hybla (major) near the south of Ætna, on a hill of the same name as the city; near it ran the Limæthus; famous for honey and bees.

Libyan flowers. Libya is the name given by the Greek and Roman poets to what is otherwise called Africa; in a more restricted sense applied to the two countries of Cyrenica and Marmarica.

71. *Tagus:* Tajo river in Portugal.

83. *streight* or strait = narrowly. *amaine* = violently.

175. *Lapithoe:* Lapithus, son of Apollo by Stilbe, brother of Centaurus.

178. *iarre* = eare, heare. *Stratmann Dict.*, p. 334.

203. Rhodope, a high mountain in Thrace.

251. Astroea, a daughter of Astræus, king of Arradia, or according to others of Titan, Saturn's brother, by Aurora; some make her daughter of Jupiter and Themis. She was called Justice as a goddess of virtue, and lived on the earth during the golden age; the impiety of mankind drove her to heaven in the brazen and iron ages, and she was placed as Virgo among the constellations of the zodiac.

NOTES TO pp. 20—32, ll. 304—623. 73

304. Atlas, a Titan, son of Japetus and Clymene, one of the Oceanides, brother of Prometheus.

305. *Heloriz:* Helorus (Abiso), a river of Sicily near the southern extremity of the island; mentioned by several ancient poets for the remarkably fertile country through which it flows. Virgil, *Æneid*, iii. 659; Ovid, *Fast.*, iv. 487.

306. Alcinous, a son of Nausithous, king of Phæacia, praised for his love of agriculture; he is the same that entertained Ulysses. Homer beautifully describes his gardens on the island of Sheria (Corfu or Corcyra).

351. *pillastrells*, from the Ital. *pillastrello*.

364. *ramillets*, from the Spanish *ramillete*, means: 1. A bunch of divers flowers and herbs tied together. 2. A collection of exquisite and useful thoughts on any subject.

Posy. 1. Motto inscribed on a ring. (Addison.) 2. A bunch of flowers. (Spenser.)

427. Lynceus, a son of Alphareus, among the hunters of the Caledonian boar, one of the Argonauts. He was so sharp-sighted, that it is reported he could see through the earth and distinguish objects at nine miles. Palaeph., 57; Pliny, ii. xvii.

451. *Gnossian Crowne:* Gnossis, Gnossia, an epithet given to Ariadne, because she lived or was born at Gnossus; the crown which she received from Bacchus, and which was made a constellation: Gnossia stella. Virgil, G. i. 222.

459—461. Hieronymus Zanchius: De operibus Dei intra spatium sex dierum creatis; Hanoviæ 1597, lib. 2, cap. 6. Thesis: Nemo Angelorum creatus fuit a Deo malus, sed omnes ex æquo boni; verum, sicut omnes intellectu ad cognoscendum præditi, sic etiam omnes voluntate ad eligendum, vel repudiandum liberi. Quare quod quidam illorum mali sint, hoc a se ipsis, non autem ex Deo habere.

582. *to cark* = to care in v. Esmay. Cf. Collier's *Old Ballads*, p. 38. F. carke = *je chagrine*. Palsgrave.

620. Phyllis, a daughter of Sitho, or according to others of Lycurgus, king of Thrace, hospitably received Demophro, son of Theseus, who at his return from the Trojan war had stopped on her coasts; became enamoured of him, and he was not insensible of her passion. After some months of mutual tenderness and affection, Demophro set sail for Athens, where his domestic affairs recalled him; promised faithfully to return as soon as a month was expired. His dislike for Phyllis, or the irreparable situation of his affairs, obliged him to violate his engagement, and Phyllis, desperate from his absence, hanged herself. Ovid, *Her.*, II. ii. 353; *Trist.*, ii. 437; Virgil, Eclogue III.

623. Pyramus, a youth of Babylon, became enamoured of Thisbe, a beautiful virgin who dwelt in the vicinity; the flame was mutual, and the two lovers, whom their parents forbade to marry, regularly received each other's addresses through the chink of a wall which separated their houses. After the most solemn vows of sincerity, they both agreed to

elude the vigilance of their friends, and meet one another on the tomb of Ninus, under a white mulberry-tree, without the walls of Babylon. Thisbe came first to the appointed place, but the sudden arrival of a lioness frightened her away; and as she fled into a neighbouring cave, dropped her veil, which the lioness found and besmeared with blood. Pyramus soon found Thisbe's veil all bloody, and concluding that she had been torn to pieces by the wild beasts of the place, stabbed himself with his sword. Thisbe, when her fears were vanished, returned from the cave, and at the sight of dying Pyramus, fell on the sword reeking with his blood. This happened under a mulberry-tree, which, as the poets mention, was stained with the blood of the lovers, and ever after bore fruit of the colour of blood. Ovid, *Met.*, iv. 55.

629. Empedocles, a philosopher, poet, and historian of Agrigentum, in Sicily, flourished in 444; he was the disciple of Telanges the Pythagorean, and warmly adopted the doctrine of transmigration. His curiosity to inspect the crater of Ætna proved fatal to him; some maintain that he wished to pass for a god, and, that his death might be unknown, threw himself into the crater; his expectations were frustrated, the volcano threw up one of his sandals, and discovered to the world that he perished by fire.

630. Stagirite, surname of Aristotle, from the city of Stagira in Macedonia, on the western shore of the Sinus Strymonicus (Gulf of Contessa), founded 665, and native place of Aristotle.

642. *sagge* = to hang down heavily (North). "Sir Rowland Russetcoat, goes sagging everie day in his round gascoynes of white cotton." —*Pierce Penilesse*, 1592.

698. *Cocyte* (Cocytus), a river of Epirus, blends its nauseous waters with those of the Achero; *Paus.*, I. 17. Its etymology, the unwholesomeness of its waters, and its vicinity to the Achero, have made the poets call it a river of hell; hence Cocytia virgo, applied to Alecto, one of the Furies. *Virg.*, G. III. 38; IV. 479. *Æneis*, VI. 297, 323; VII. 479.

700. *scritch* = to shriek (Devonshire).

711. Amphitrite, daughter of Oceanus and Thetis, married Neptune, though he had made a vow of perpetual celibacy; she had a statue at Corinth in the temple of Neptune, sometimes called Salaria, often taken for the sea itself. Ovid, *Met.*, i. 14.

720, 722. It looks, at first, as if these lines needed transposing; but the point is, that the folk in Hell suffer at the same moment both intense heat and intense cold, and yet neither of these affords any relief to its opposite.

759—66. H. Zanchius, De operibus, etc., lib. 4, cap. 19. Thesis: Dæmones sive præditi sint corporibus, sive non præditi: Tamen præter spiritualem montis et voluntatis multiplicem afflictionem, tormentum etiam ac dolorem, et nunc a multis rebus corporeis pati, idque mirabilibus modis possibile est atque probabile: Et postmodum a fine seculi usque in sempiternum passuros esse ab igne Gebennali necesse est.

767. Cimmerii, a people near the Palus Mæotis; invaded Asia

Minor, and seized on the kingdom of Cyaxares; masters of the country for 28 years; driven back by Algathes, king of Lydia (Herod., I. vi. 4). They seem to have been a northern nation driven from their abodes by the Scythians, and compelled to seek for new habitations; Posidonius makes them of Cimbric or German origin. Their first appellation is not known; that of Cimmerii they are said to have obtained after inhabiting the town of Cimmerium and its vicinity on the Cimmerian Bosporus. This seems improbable, as it is more natural to suppose that they gave name to the town and strait. The country bordering on the Palus Mæotis and Bosporus, inhabited by the Cimmerii, is represented by the ancients as inhospitable and black, covered with forests and fogs, impenetrable for the sun; hence, according to some, arose the expression Cimmerian darkness. Homer places his Cimmerium beyond the Oceanus, in a land of continual gloom, and immediately after them the empire of the shades.

773. *Leviathan* (Hebrew): water animal mentioned in the book of Job, by some imagined to be the crocodile, but in poetry generally taken for the whale. No known animal answers to it exactly. Shakspere mentions it in *Henry V.*, III. iii. Compare Job xii.

789. *fecche* = to fetch.

815. Cynthus (Monte Cintio), a mountain of Delos. Apollo was surnamed Cynthius; Diana, Cynthia; as born on the mountain sacred to them. Virgil, G. iii. 36; Ovid, *Met.*, vi. 304.

818. Cynosure (Cape Cavala), a promontory of Attica, formed by the range of Pentelicus.

820. Phlegetho, a river of hell whose waters were burning. Virgil, *Æneid*, vi. 550; Ovid, *Met.*, xv. 532.

829. Tityus, a giant, son of Terra, according to others of Jupiter by Elara, daughter of Orchomenos, was of such a prodigious size, that his mother died in travail after Jupiter had drawn her from the bowels of the earth, where she had been concealed during her pregnancy, to avoid the anger of Juno. Ovid, *Met.*, iv. 457.

834. Ixion, king of Thessaly, was tortured in hell by being tied to a wheel which was continually whirling round. Virgil, *Æneid*, vi. 601; Ovid, *Met.*, xii. 210, 338.

870. Vergellus, a small river near Cannæ, falling into the Aufidus, over which Hannibal (the Punicki) made a bridge with the slaughtered bodies of the Romans. Flor., ii. 6.

871. Perillus, an artist of Athens, made a brazen bull for Phalaris, tyrant of Agrigentum. This machine was fabricated to put criminals to death by burning them alive, and it was said that their cries were like the roaring of a bull. When Perillus gave it to Phalaris, the tyrant made the first experiment on him, and cruelly put him to death by lighting a slow fire under the belly of the bull. Pliny, xxxiv. 8; Ovid, *A. A.*, i. 439, 653.

959—966. H. Zanchius, De operibus, etc., lib. 3, cap. 9. Thesis: Quæ in nobis sunt cogitationes, desideria et affectus, nisi per externa vel affecta, vel signa sese utcumque prodant, vel a Deo revelentur: cognosci ab Angelis minime possunt. lib. 4, cap. 9. (The manuscript gives wrongly lib. 9, for the book contains but five chapters.) Thesis: Dæmones nullas hominis cogitationes certo et per se cognoscere possunt; sed multas per externa signa et probabiliter percipere valent.

1011. Panopee, one of the Nereides, whom sailors generally invoked in storms. Virgil, *Æneid*, v. 825.

1124. Castalus fons in Syria, near Daphne; the waters believed to give a knowledge of futurity to those who drank them. The oracle at the fountain promised Hadrian supreme power when he was yet in a private station; he had the fountain shut up with stones when he ascended the throne.

1574. "*Better maye hee that sange his birth, ringe out his knell.*" The Singer of Christ's birth, referred to in this line, is doubtless Thomas Becon (or Beacon), born about 1512 in Norfolk or Suffolk, and died in 1567 or 1570. He is a contemporary of, and most likely a man well known to, Robinson. I have mentioned in the introduction that Robinson belonged to the divines who were ordered to assist Bishop Cranmer in the compilation of the Book of Common Prayer. Becon was Cranmer's chaplain, and Prebendary of Canterbury; he was a learned divine, and published a great number of writings of a religious character, which appeared in three folio volumes in 1560—4. News about his life may be gained from—1. Lupton's *History of the Modern Protestant Divines*. Lond. 1637. 2. The Biographies prefixed to the late selections of his writings published by the Religious Tract Society (*British Reformers*. Lond. 1828—31), and by the Society for Promoting Christian Knowledge (*Selections from the Works of Thomas Becon.* Lond. 1839). 3. Several particulars may also be gleaned from *Fox* and *Strype.* A complete list of his numerous writings is to be found in Tanner's *Bibliotheca Britannica*. The Rev. John Ayre, M.A., republished most of Becon's works in 1844 (Cambridge) for the Parker Society, and prefixed to his edition the little that is known about Becon's life. The poem in question is entitled: "A newe Dialoge betwene thangel of god and the Shepherds of ye felde concerning the nativite & byrth of Iesus Christ our Lord and savior, no lesse Godly than swete and pleasante to reade, lately compyled by Thomas Becon." It is the only known poetical work of the author, and not yet republished; it appears that it is very little known, and even Allibone does not mention it under Becon. The first stanza runs:

> A swete message
> To euery age
> From God so sage
> Is gyuen to me:
> Whiche to declare
> Both nere and fare
> To exclude care
> Glad wolde I be, etc.

INDEX OF NAMES, WORDS, AND SUBJECTS.

The numbers refer to the pages (and lines, when like 10/33) in the text.

Words marked by an asterisk (*) are to be found in the notes.

ACHERON, 9, 29, 46.
Ægeus, 32.
Ætna, 32, 37.
Agglad, 20, 21, 30, 47, 66/1559.
Aggrate, vb. delight, 22/343.
Aiax, 32.
Alcides, 11.
*Alcinous, 20.
Allmightie, 50.
Aloe, 47.
Amber. 10, 11, 13, 15.
Ambition, 33.
Ambrosia, 17.
Ambrosian mercy, 29/541.
Amos, 26.
Amphion, 4.
*Amphitrite, 35.
Andromede, 46.
Antiques (Ancients), 17/216.
Antony, 32.
Aphrodite, 11, 12, 19, 56.
Apollo, 11, 22.
Apostrophe (to Christ), 64.
Appendix, 10/33.
*Aratus, 5.
Arctos, 26.
Aristoteles, 26, 32.
Aspiring, a. 25/416.
Assyrian (Spikenard), 12.
*Astroea, 18, 43, 52.
Atlas, 16.
Ayre, 26.

BACCUS, 11, 14, 22.
Besiluered, 22/355.
Bespread, 57/1306.
*Birth, Christ's, 66.
  — Marie's, 9.
Braine-sicke, 15/172.
Brothers twaine, 26.

CABINETS, 61/1430.
Cain, 40.
Calamus, 47.
Camphire, 47.
Candle, 26.
Cannon, 40/873.
Canticles, 43, 44, 47, 49.
Captiuated eyes, 47/1052.
Carking care, 50/582.
Carnation, 22.
Carthagenian Queen, 32.
Casia, 21, 44.
Cassiope, 26.
*Castalian plaine, 50.
Catamite, 13/118.
Cato, 32.
Catullus, 5.
Cedars, 47.
Centaures, 15.
Charret, 11/45.
Chaucer, 4.
Chevisaunce, a flower, 21/317.
Christ, 42, 43, 44, 46, 53, 61, 63, 64, 66, 67.
Chrysolite, 26, 44.
*Chrysostome, 6.
Chrystall (Christall), 10, 21, 35, 52, 57.
*Cimmerian (mistes), 37.
Cinnamon, 47.
Circe, 16, 18.
Cleared, a. 16/182.
Cleopatra, 14, 32.
Close-throng'd prease, 35/717.
Cloves (of Paradise), 21.
Cockell, 32.
*Cocyte, 34.
Cogitations, 57/1313.
Colchos, 14/137.
Columbine, 21.

INDEX OF NAMES, WORDS, AND SUBJECTS.

Comets, 27.
Comparison, 15.
Compasse, fecches, 37/789.
Conceitinge, fancying, 38/824.
Congeald, 39/826.
Conscience, 25, 41, 46, 55.
Couslips of Hierusalem, 21/324.
Crinkled snake, 30/567.
Crocodile, 29, 41, 55.
Cronicles, 3.
*Crowne (Gnossian), 26.
Cupid, 23, 28.
Custom, 29, st. 63.
Cydney (Sidney), 4.
*Cynosure, 38/818.
*Cynthia, 26, 28.
Cyprian Queen, 56.

DAEDALEAN gyre, 35.
Daffodill, 21.
Daine, deign, vouchsafe, 10/19.
Danaus, 39.
Darnell, 32.
Darte, 26.
Death of Christ, 67.
— of Mary, 9/4.
Debared, bare, 17/223.
Debarred, 41.
*Debellished, 9.
Debonaire, 16.
Declininge, a. ? 3/375.
Deglorious, 18/241.
Delicates, 14/149.
Deludinge, 20/302.
Depraved, 22 ; 27/475.
Deprostrate, 12/77.
Depurpured, 17/228.
Descants, delights, 23/372.
Despaire, 13.
Destinies, 50.
Diamonds, 10.
Diana, 18.
Dido, 32.
Dimure, 20/291.
Disodour'd, 60/1387.
Dispreads, 47/1045.
Dissheueled haire, 38/805.
Dizieth, 11/53.
Dominations, 36/759.
Dotingely, 20/291.
Dragon, 26.
Drones, 18.
Dryades, 14.
Dutifully, 43/931.

EAGLE, 9, 25.
Eglantine, 21.
Elegiacks, 3.
Elegies, 4.
Elephants, 11.
Elysian fields, 14.
Embait, 29/531.
Embellish'd, 16/199.
Emblem, 3.
*Empedocles, 6.
Enamouringe, 21/327.
Enchauntresse, 13/101.
Encomiasticks, 4/25.
Enuie, 13.
Epigrammes, 3.
Epitaphe, 3.
Ethnicke Poetry, 3/18.
Euhoe, 38.
Ezekiel, 26.

FALERN wine, 12.
Famine, 29.
Fantasticke, 34/689.
Fate, 25, 36.
Fauereous yewe, 32/619.
*Fecche, 37.
Festered, a. 27/476.
Flaggy, a. 18/238.
Flashinge lightninges, 45/976.
Flattery, 12.
Fleece (the golden), 14.
Flitting, 12/88.
Flittinge dayes, 58/1328.
Fluent, 17/212.
Flute, 15.
Flutteringe bat, 31/613.
Fondling, n. 27/479.
Foolish Laughter, 12.
Fosterer, 48/1081.
Franticke, 32.

GARDEN (of Pleasure), 20.
Gilead, 49, 63.
Gilly-flower, 22/357.
Glimmeringe, n. 37/769.
Glories = God's, 26/446.
Glow-worm, 55.
Gluttonie, 14.
Goblet, 26.
Gods, 5.
Golgotha, 66.
Gorgon, 16, 31, 33.
*Gnossian Crowne, 26/451.
Graces, 13.

INDEX OF NAMES, WORDS, AND SUBJECTS.

Grapelets, 17/219.
Greeces, steps, 10/41.
Grimme-fac'd cat, 31/612.
Griping, *a.* 28/525.
Ground-worke, foundation, 48/1058.
Gyre, *n.* 35/707.

HAIRE, 26.
Halleluiah, 56.
Haltinge sacrifice, 24/406.
Hannibal, 40.
*Harrington, 5.
Heaven, 26.
Hector, 6.
Helicon, 4.
Hell, 25, 34, 35, 46, 56, 66.
Hellen, 14, 26.
*Heloriz, 20.
Helpinge hand, 48/1078.
Hermitinge humility, 65/1525.
Hermon, 44.
Hero, 3.
Hesiod, 6.
Hesperides, 16.
Hierarchies, 36/759.
Hight, 19.
Homer, 6, 37.
Horace, 6.
Humility, 48.
Hyæna-like, 32/637.
*Hybla (Thyme of), 13.
Hypothesis, 9.

IBIS, 41, 52.
Idlenesse, 13.
Illumined, 53/1216.
Imbezilinge, 15/160.
Immanteled, 25/425.
Imu'd, 18/248.
Inconstancie, 13.
Indian treasure, 12.
Interchast, 10/37.
Inuegled, 35/730.
Inveild, 9/5.
Invocation (the poet's), 10.
Ire, 27, 36.
Isicles, tears, 58/1354.
Ivory, 16/200, 44/945; white feet, 62/1458.
*Ixion, 39.

*JARRE, *vb.* 16/178.
Iazynths, 10.

Jealousy, 13.
Jehova, 24, 50.
Jerusalem, 27.
Jesus. *See* Christ.
Jett, 11, 16, 19.
John, 67.
Jollity, 30/578; jollities, 38/800.
Jolly, 19/255.
Jove, 4, 33.
Junonian plumes, 28/502.

LABYRINTHS, 48.
Laeander, 3.
Lambkins, 11/60.
Languishement, 24/388.
*Lapithoe, 15.
Lasciuious, 56/1293.
Laughter (foolish), 12.
Laureat, *a.* 4/37.
Lawny, 28/519.
Leauy, 42/906.
Lebanon, 47, 63.
Leige-Lord, 66.
Lethargy, 17.
*Leviathan, 37.
Levite, 27.
Libellize, 4/27.
Liberality, 63.
Lilie, 22.
Limber strookes, 37/787; strawes, 39/851.
*Lucan, 5.
Lucifer, 41.
Luke, 43.
Lute, 13, 15.
Luxury, 12, 16, 23.
*Lybian flore, 12.
Lydian wealth, 12.
*Lynceus, 25/427.

MARY MAGDALENE:
— her beauty, 16, 56.
— her tongue, lips, brows, cheeks, nose, bare breasts, 17.
— her hands, legs and feet, heart, 18.
— her lover, 20.
— her arbour, 22.
— her sorrows, 28.
— in Melancholie's cave, 33.
— tormented by seven Spirits, 36, 37.
— her fancy disordered, 38.

INDEX OF NAMES, WORDS, AND SUBJECTS.

Mary Magdalene:
— rescued by Christ, 46.
— guided to the Palace of Wisdom, 47.
— her repentance in teares, in gesture, in sorrowful eiaculations and in laments . . . 54.
— acknowledginge her former misdemeanour . . . . . 56.
— in humblenesse and detestinge her former sinful life, 57.
— in contemplation, 59.
— in her wishes, 60.
— in her behaviour and her charity, 62.
— reflections on her acts, 63.
— in her religious duties, 66.
— in her sorrow for Iesus' death, 67.
— tells the Saints the resurrection of Christ, 68.
Margarites, 47.
Marigold, 21, 42.
Massy, 48/1058.
Medusa, 16, 31.
Melancholy, his cave, 31.
— his gesture, 32.
— the parts of his body, 32.
— his apparell, 32.
— diverse kinds of, 33.
Meltinge soules, 23/374.
Menades, 38.
Messias, 44.
Mickle, 59/1370.
Militants, 53/1204.
Milke-white, 45/991.
Mithridates, 40.
Moecenas, 6/106.
Moecenases, *pl.* patrons, 6/105.
Monarch (of England), 50.
Moses, 6.
Musaeus, 3.
Muse, 7, 23, 51.
Myrrhe, 43, 47.
Myrtle, 11, 58.

NAIADES, 14.
Narcissus, 21, 22.
Nectar, 12, 17, 64.
Nemesis, 35, 36.
Neptune, 14.
Neptunian, 18/238.

Nereides, 18.
Nile, 40.
Nummed ghost, 61/1434.

OCEAN, 15.
Ore (Gold), 13, 47.
Outrun, 67/1584.
Outstrip, 26/459; 67/1594.
Ovid, 5, 29, 34.
Oyntinge, anointing, 64/1518.

PAENITENCE. *See* Repentance.
Palace of Pleasure, 10, 11, 29.
— of Wisdom, 48.
Palate-pleasinge, 28/520.
*Panopee, 46.
Parable of debt, 65.
Paradise, 21, 25, 27, 52, 68.
Paragon, 13/95; 67.
Paramour, 14, 21.
Pastorall, 3.
Paunce, pansy ?, 21/316.
Perfumed, *a.* 21/318.
Perfumes, 47.
*Perillus, 40.
Perseus, 31, 46.
*Persius, 4.
Peter, 67.
Pharise, 60, 61, 62, 65.
*Phlegetonticko maine, 38/820.
Phosphorus, 42.
*Phyllis, 32.
*Pillastrell, 40/351.
Pinke, 21.
Pitchy, 30/560.
Plato, 3.
Pleasure, 10, 11, 23, 29, 57.
Pleiades, 26.
Pliny, 32.
Plume, 24.
Plump, 12/82.
Pluto, 31, 38.
Poetry, Ethnicke, 3.
Polluted, *a.* 23/367.
Pome-granates, 13, 47, 49.
*Posies, 23.
Postes, *vb.* hastes, 68/1623.
Pride, 12.
Primrose, 21.
Proesumption, 13.
Proëuents, goes before, 67/1582.
Propertius, 4.
Prophet, 65.
Prostitute, *a.* 14/143.

INDEX OF NAMES, WORDS, AND SUBJECTS. 81

*Prudentius, 6.
Punick (Hannibal), 40.
Pursive, 12/82.
Putrefaction, 52/1193.
*Pyramus, 32.

QUIETNESSE, 46/1016.
Quintessence, 50.
Quivering, a. 28/511.

*RAMILLETS, 23/364.
Rapsodie, 7/110.
Rasters (? rafters), 26/456; 49/1088.
Refind, 10/29.
Rejecter, 50/1115.
Repentance, 46, 47, 52.
— closet, actions, attire, attendants, 51.
— her river of teares, 52.
— the only way to life, 52.
Resplendent, 26/465.
Revelation, 26.
*Rhodope, 16.
Riualdry, 33/648.
Rivelets, 19/267.
Roses, 21, 22.

SAFFRON, 47.
Sagge, vb. 32/642.
Salomon, 6, 50.
— Wisdom, 49, 50.
Saltest brine, 67/1599.
Sappheires, 10, 44.
Satyres, 3, 4.
Saviour, 53, 61, 63, 64.
Scaldinge fire, 34/704.
Scorpions, 37.
*Scritch, 34.
Scund'd, 37/766.
Scylla, 31, 40.
Scythian, 40.
Self-hate, 63.
Sences, 44.
Seneca, 27.
*Shaggy, 30.
Shined, perf. t. 25/430.
Sidney, the poet, 4.
Sieve-like, 39/837.
Simeon, 6, 62, 65.
Sirens, 55.
Sisyphus, 39.
Slowe-pac'd asse, 31/613.
Snale-like pace, 32/641.
Snowy, 13/119.

MARY MAGDALENE.

Sol (Sun), 11, 14, 19, 23, 29.
Song (of the Goddess of Pleasure), 13.
*Song of Christ's birth, 66.
Soundinge, swooning, 45/986.
Spanish friar, 40.
Speare, 26.
Sphoere, 26.
Spikenard, 12/72.
Spiny, 9/7.
Sportefull, 22/337.
Squared, 10/41.
*Stagirite (Aristoteles), 32.
Steeled, a. 19/259.
Steepy, 11/59.
Steepy, 34/695; 39/833; 42/907.
Stole, n. robe, 9/10.
Submissely, 25/424.
Sulphurean sent, 36/758.
Stygian vassals, 36.
Sweltred, a. 24/392.
Syneide, Conscience, 35, 41, 46, 55.

TAGUS (gemms of), 12.
— (sand of), 14.
Tartary, 36.
Teares, 52, st. 143.
— river of, 52.
Thetis, 14.
Throughes, throws, 20/301.
*Thyme of Hybla, 12.
Thysbe, 32.
Tiffany, 25/423.
Timbrell, 15.
Tinne-decayinge, 47/1050.
Titan, 16, 19, 33.
*Tityus, 39.
Tressels, legs, 18/232; 63/1471.
Tricklinge teares, 51/1153.
Tripple Isle, Monarch of, 50/1132.
Troian, 14.
Turrulet, 11/49.
Twinkling of an eye, 27/473.
Tyber, 40.

UNCTION, 63/1468.
Undivided, 44/952.
Unexpected, 60/1410.
Unsounded, 29/534.
Uprent, 11/48.

VALE (lily of the), 22.
Valted, a. 15/165.
Veluet leaues, 21/331.

G

Venus, 11, 12, 17, 19, 56.
*Vergell, 40.
Vestaes sonnes, 23/378.
Violetts, 21, 22.
Vipereous, 29/547 ; 30/565.
Virgil, 5, 30, 37.
Virgin waxe, 16/197.

WANTONESSE, 12, 23.
Wantonize, 24/404.
Ware, n. 16/181.
Waueringe Thomas, 64/1519.
Wine, 15/173-4.
Wisdom, 46.

Wisdoms forrest, 47.
— palace and tower, 48.
— riches, 49.
— properties and chambers, 50
Wreathed chaine, 30/568.

YCHARM'D, 61/1438.
Yclinge, vb. 22/339.
Younglinges, 40/856.
Ysprout, vb. 22/349.

*ZANCHIUS, 26, 36, 44.
Zephyre, 21.

The manufacturer's authorised representative in the EU for product safety is Oxford University Press España S.A. of El Parque Empresarial San Fernando de Henares, Avenida de Castilla, 2 - 28830 Madrid (www.oup.es/en or product.safety@oup.com). OUP España S.A. also acts as importer into Spain of products made by the manufacturer.

Printed and bound by CPI Group (UK) Ltd, Croydon, CR0 4YY

02/04/2026

02083219-0004